Twenty-two Days
or Half a Lifetime

Twenty-two Days
or Half a Lifetime

Franz Fühmann

*Translated from the German
by Leila Vennewitz*

JONATHAN CAPE
LONDON

First published in Great Britain 1992
English translation © Seven Seas Publishers, Berlin, 1980
First published in German under the title
Zweiundzwanzig Tage oder Die Hälfte des Lebens
© by Hinstorff Verlag, Rostock, in 1973
Jonathan Cape, 20 Vauxhall Bridge Road, London SW1V 2SA

A CIP catalogue record for this book is available from
the British Library

ISBN 0-224-03339-5

Printed in Great Britain by
St Edmundsbury Press, Bury St Edmunds, Suffolk

Twenty-two Days
or Half a Lifetime

Berlin, East Station, Platform A, North-South Express,
23:45 – the night-time atmosphere of this station seems, as
always, nice and snug: the night is black and the lights are
subdued, the sky is a vault of iron over solid ground, with
pigeons sleeping in safe nests. Little clouds drift by, milk-
white and plump, tame dragons snort in their harness, and
what otherwise would be wolf and sheep, lion and lamb,
leopard and gazelle, lies in close embrace, free from fear
or suspicion, each with the other's welfare at heart. God is
near and accessible, His order intelligible, the archangel
wears a red cap, the guardian angel a red sash, the snake
shall not enter here, and even He with the sooty face
performs a useful service. O brave, sound world

Perhaps a few palm trees should be installed

National character reflected in leave-taking. I believe the
German feels purified

Obsessive fear: having to share a compartment with
someone who has just completed his doctoral thesis on
"The Epic Theater, and Bertolt Brecht as Dramatist."
Sigh of relief: the other bed has not been let down

Next door in the open compartment: two generals, their
collars unbuttoned. One is reading the newspaper – a very
strange sight. A book would be conceivable and within the
tradition. A newspaper seems all wrong. Why?
(I think I know

and of course immediately a memory: the general inside
the kasha cauldron in the POW camp. It being his turn to

scrape out the remainder, he had crawled in head first, and so far in that all you could see – against the vacant, dun-colored horizon – were his legs with the red piping; after that I ceased to think of generals as gods

Ejaculatio praecox of a handkerchief unfolding even before the train has got under way

The hand of the station clock does not glide, it hops from minute to minute, and so conscientiously that its movement seems profoundly soothing

On the platform, mentally spitting on the palms of their hands, appear two cleaning women with giant brooms (maybe an idea for my *Prometheus*: at the end of Mekone

As I see him, Poseidon often has the look of a station-master; Apollo would be quite credible in that role, Hermes and Ares barely, Hephaistos, Hades, Dionysos not at all. Zeus least of all: that function would be quite beyond his capability

Nor Prometheus, he would just play around. ... But Epimetheus would be ideal for the part

Interior with genuine clouds

A shrill whistle like the crack of a liontamer's whip, and beyond my window the station wall glides back sound-lessly, the way it was trained

Startled sparks

Down the corridor a tall young Romanian woman, blue-black coat under a midnight-blue silk scarf over blue-black hair above blue-and-black-shadowed eyes, and on the platform a weedy, seedy-looking man of indeterminate age, tongue-tied by emotion, swaying on his toes and supported by two swaying companions, blows a boozy kiss into the white steam, a kiss which the woman, with a sudden sob, does not return

"A beautiful human being is really only beautiful for an instant" – wherever did I read those terrible words

Steel wheels purring like cats

and midnight comes on the dot. ... A glance at the clock confirms that time is punctual to the second! O brave, sound world

Weird thought, that each day starts with midnight, the phantom hour, the hour from twelve to one. But weirder still is the discovery that this isn't so at all: midnight does not start at O, it starts at 24 hours, that's it. ... The old day glides into the new one, the momentary point in time stands still for a whole hour, for a little while today remains yesterday – and the dead groan in their graves, and the wakeful, fearful dogs howl

A point in time – what is it? Dimensionless time, how are we to conceive it? Dimensionless space, the dot, is the intersection of two one-dimensional entities – but what intersects the line of time? The meridian? That intersects the projection of the course of the sun. A second, different time-line? But how are we to conceive it, and, supposing it to be conceivable, *how* are we to conceive it? And: can a point in time exist, even for a mere flash, in the same way that a point in space exists? Surely it is only what is to come or what is already past, the middle between two boundaries which collide without a middle: no present tense (hence no preterit either). Would there be any languages that have such verbs, i.e., with future and past only

Yet the adverb for this absence of the present is "now" (like "there" for the absence of space) and that is a mystery

Intersecting lines – the sadists' club in geometry

Perhaps the strange thing about that good-bye scene five minutes ago was that it was a woman who was saying good-bye – in the sense of going away. This is a new, as yet undeveloped mythologem – traditionally it being always the men who leave the women, at least as far as I know. Ariadne goes back, not away; Helen is carried off, and when Kore says farewell she is not leaving her husband, she is leaving her mother

Books to read when traveling: according to an approved rule of thumb one should always choose something in contrast – for a trip to the Crimea, for instance, an account of a North Pole expedition. So what do you choose for a trip to Hungary, that intersection of every imaginable historical and spiritual line? I searched for a long time, constantly rejecting; I was about to take along the Bible but finally decided on Jean Paul: *Army Chaplain Attila Schmelzle's Journey to Flätz* – it seems to me that, in spite of the name Attila, it must offer that something Other, a contrast to Hungary

Comically grotesque the notion for a story, a nasty idea, and suddenly, as if smitten by an avenging fist, fatigue

Falling asleep in the moving train: memories of long ago, perhaps of those earliest youthful hiking groups, muffled tramping of many hundreds of feet, lulling rhythms, flitting darkness and gentle swaying, murmur of strange yet familiar sounds, then the thrust and pull of centrifugal force – so oddly disembodied yet so distinct in its grip and guidance of hips and shoulders – as the train rounds the curves into the unknown

After passport and customs, customs and passport and long, dreamless sleep: where are we? An embankment, above it only the tops of a few young pine trees, all dignity and headlong rush under the uniformly gray sky – where

In the mirror of the cabinet over the washbasin the scenery proceeds in reverse to the movement offered the eye through the window, and if outside it seems to be running away from you, in the mirror it is coming toward you. The future manifests itself as the present; form and duration of the world outside are doubled: a magical gain, but this duplication also causes vertigo, one is no longer sure of one's place; the question of forward or backward becomes meaningless, and at the line where mirror and window meet the divided world runs together, flowing into itself and canceling itself out: antimatter and matter soundlessly meeting in a shimmer, each soundlessly destroying itself in the other

Does the future exist in every now? Apparently

Chalk-white, moon-white: kilometer stones beside the dark-green forest beyond the marshy meadow: wolf's teeth in a whale's maw. Each white spot, lasting hardly ten train-seconds, catches my eye, and each time I know that it is becoming monotonous, yet I continue to look out for a long time

Bratislava: four soldiers sipping glasses of beer as they run, and behind them a frail little woman hurrying along with a huge teddy bear lying between the handles of her holdall, a strange Pietà, strange also in its movement

Women puffing cigarettes: we are approaching Hungary

Two peasant girls with umbrellas

Strange apparition at a railway station: a chimney sweep with ladder, iron ball, and top hat. Why is this so startling, alarming even? An American Indian in full war regalia would surprise but not startle. It isn't the confusion of geographical elements that bewilders us but the confusion of functions. It is not the exotic stranger who makes us feel uneasy but the person whose function, real or intended, we do not know – Hoffmann's privy councilors, for example, or, in the passive tense, Gogol's document copiers

Dirt, as we know, is matter in the wrong place. Would fright be a wrong functioning? That would also explain its proximity to laughter

Beyond the station among swarms of crows, myriads of brown and gray scraps of paper like miniature kites, mounting or diving through the air in tiny jerks, frighteningly malevolent

A last salute from Slovakia: a row of green-roofed, colorful beehives, the fronts blue, green, red, yellow in every combination like the flags of all nations, a buzzing peaceful co-existence! And one more salute: beside a field of maize, a sky-blue motorcar, surrounded by playful white chickens, with two pheasants solemnly stalking by

No longer in the one country, not yet in the other: three hours' delay! There's your middle between two borders! And I had deliberately chosen this (uncomfortable) train so that I could begin the little travel book I am planning with a description of Esztergom above the Danube at dusk

The dual meaning of the word "stalk" is quite amusing, e.g., to express a disappointment:

> I'd hoped to see some pheasants stalk
> But there was just a cabbage stalk

Odd. There must be some significance behind such like-sounding words

To be written (maybe at the Széchenyi baths): a slim volume of poetry where the title would always be longer than the corresponding poem

Budapest, Western Station, taxi rank, mud and rain. A grimy, tipsy and altogether disagreeable bum lends an unsolicited hand in loading the baggage; he is made to realize that he is not wanted, and if he should still succeed in snatching up a suitcase and stuffing it in the trunk, his begging hand thrust deep into the car would be ignored. I too am determined not to accept any help, and so obviously is Gábor, but Elga allows him to stow away her shopping bag and gives him something as she gets into the car. "Never mind," she says in response to my reproachful surprise. "Never mind, just a few forints," and in a conciliatory voice, before I can scold her: "Didn't you notice? He badly needs a drink, and he's still short three or four forints for a bottle, so he lends a hand with the baggage, and now he's happy!" "Some happiness!" I say angrily, and Elga replies that happiness is happiness, it has nothing to do with any moral code, at best with the legal code, and what a new book means to me is what his bottle will mean to him tonight! I growl in irritation; Gábor smiles to himself as usual, and Elga says, nodding in my direction: "Don't forget he's come straight from Prussia!" But at that moment we draw up at the Astoria

What makes these turn-of-the-century hotels so enchanting is their kinship with the Sesame cave. Although in many ways they are its opposite (for instance, they stand out from the surrounding rock piles instead of blending with them, and emphasize their entrance instead of making it invisible), they belong to the realm of Ali Baba and Sindbad. The Duna Continental or the Stadt Berlin or the Havana Hilton would never prompt such ideas; although without the slightest connection to any fairy tale, they do have something in common with a fully automated chicken factory. Something that cannot function any other way than it does is not a fairy tale, but here we are in the sphere of magic and so we willingly put up with some discomfort, like now, for instance: for the first week with a makeshift room (Interhotels wouldn't have such a thing

Astoria: at the reception desk, every telephone of a different color (red, green, brown, white); outside the manager's office a life-size bronze centaur is wrestling with a Lapith, and behind them the manager, ensconced in marble and stucco, writes surrealistic poems – could my hosts, the Magyar P.E.N. Club, have chosen better headquarters for me

And in my room the wardrobe: a chamber designed by Frankenstein or Meyrink, an oaken dungeon, an Anak's coffin, a Goliath's cubbyhole: ten feet high, six feet wide, three feet deep, no shelves, and clear across the cavernous interior a rod as thick as your arm, and a bolt suitable for Bluebeard's seventh door. But this bolt is on the inside, not on the outside, and anyone guessing the Open Sesame of its secret would experience the thousand-and-second night

Gábor is waiting; I had a yen for some fish soup, spicy and with real paprika, so the hotel restaurant wouldn't do, and the delighted Gábor begins reeling off the bistros, but then when I add to my demands: "And hot, you know, really hot, not just lukewarm, but straight from the hot stove to the table," even he frowns with concern. "How can you eat anything so bad for you?" he asks. "It's enough to burn your guts

There are a hundred reasons in favor of Hungarian cooking, the first being that it tastes good. And four reasons against it: not enough vegetables; everything cooked in lard; often lukewarm; and, most of all, it tastes *too* good

The famous restaurant famous for its game was overcrowded. We might have found two seats at a table for four, but it is considered tactless to disturb couples or friends in conversation. Here the desire to spend one's evening undisturbed includes the willingness to grant others the same right, and this habit has even rubbed off on my own compatriots. ... True, there is a dearth of housing and a plethora of restaurants, but the whole attitude is different: life is more public and at the same time more private than, say, in Berlin or Erfurt; there one excludes the other, whereas here the two extremes postulate each other. In restaurant or café, you take your time and no one minds, no waiter presses you to keep ordering, those waiting for tables do so without grumbling or pushing, and anyone who, like us, is genuinely hungry or in a hurry is free to find another place a few doors away

And in the very next restaurant there is room, lots of room, we are almost alone in the dining section. Eight tables, only two of them occupied, and fish soup is served – no, specially prepared according to Gábor's instructions, fish soup ("Where?" Elga will ask eagerly tomorrow morning.

"Real fish soup? Spicy? Hot? In Pest? Impossible!" – and she'll be right, for we're in Buda!). Fish soup, then, a steaming devil's cauldron which, in spite of all the pungent spices, neither numbs nor corrodes the palate. The carp is firm, snow-white, neither mossy nor overcooked yet light and tasting as if it had fed all its life only on nuts, and the waiter in charge of our table announces in a tone that would turn any contradiction into an insult: "And after that, gentlemen, you will have cottage-cheese dumplings, I've already ordered them in the kitchen!" Up here the lighting is dim but, what a relief, no orchestra, for a few steps lower down people are playing cards, a well-lit, large plain room, almost square, with white wooden tables; bright lights under green shades; they are playing with concentration, silently, scarcely a comment, no arguing, the kibitzers say nothing, there are hardly any women. There is little drinking; they are playing for money, of course, intently of course, no games of chance of course: vint, tarok, bezique, sixty-six. The money in little piles beside each player clinks softly, the kibitzers say nothing; the waiters move about soundlessly; at one of the tables a very pretty mascot-girl stares in fascination at the cards lying on the table

A fine drizzle on the way back to the hotel: on the Danube the reflected lights flow together to form great trembling colorful patches; in the rain the flowers open up, great big flowers filling the Danube, a blossoming gray below the black hill, in the center of which, brilliantly illuminated, stands Saint Gellért, Budapest's censorious patron saint

A program for my next three weeks would be set up to-morrow, says Gábor – experience has shown that P.E.N. Club's program will be humane, and as far as I am concerned I have none. I have in mind a little book of travel notes, something random, varied, not even limited to Hungary, a kind of extended diary, and that I keep anyway each evening. I have long since finished my translations of Füst; for the time being the first quarter of my *Prometheus* is completed, and in my suitcase I have a few verbatim translations of the later poems of József plus a Hungarian grammar and a Hungarian textbook. All I ask for is peace, a chance to daydream, loaf, do nothing, stroll about, browse in antiquarian bookstores, in other words: be on vacation. Frankly, I won't be able to stand it for more than three days even here, but that would be something at least

And a final glance into the wardrobe: is Kazim sitting in there, or even Marjanah? The bolt gleams ... and way down at the bottom something rustles: a little mouse

And sleep

October 16

Although this is my third visit to Budapest, my first steps
outside the building are still steps taken in a totally strange
city. No – no longer totally strange, I know the main streets
and the public transportation, I can just about make myself
understood, decipher signs, notice boards, even the framed
menus hanging outside the restaurants; I can understand
a few words and idioms, yet in sound, and even in spite
of the Latin alphabet, this language is of such consistent
Otherness that I can sympathize with the hapless immi-
grant: on the lookout for a readable line, on the alert for
a familiar sound, and then you hear familiar sounds and
discover you have understood a line because you read it
the day before yesterday and escape head over heels into
the Other

Two elderly gentlemen, silver-haired and befurred, suddenly abandoning their dignity, hail each other lustily
across the street, their upflung hands, gesticulating wildly
above their leathery, beaming faces, suddenly wipe out the
present: two Hun horsemen meeting on the desolate steppe

"What you are seeing is only the surface, mind you!"
I know that, but what else can I see! One has to be prepared at least to take it in and, just because it is the surface
of the essence, to recognize it as essential. Then, when observed, this surface will reveal much and, when thought
out, will point to almost everything. Even the surface built
around a fictional entity is revealing. Last year when I was
in the *puszta*, in the Hortobágy: in response to a signal,
the young fellows in their black leather jackets and metal-
studded pants who were drinking Cola and beer, moved
their motorbikes out of the way, dressed themselves up as

csikós, the traditional horse herdsmen, and, striking appropriate poses, prepared to perform those stagey folklore dances for the benefit of the tourists from Nevada who were out to get a taste of the real Hungary. There was even provision, so I was told, for encountering bandits, brandishing knives as they surrounded the bus, sinister horsemen threatening kidnaping and rape who fortunately, in the very act of reaching for jewelry and wallets, are persuaded to discuss terms of ransom and finally gallop off across the fields in a cloud of dust, back to the motel, the sound of beat music, and the greedy cash register of the travel agency. ... The bored expertise of the performers was evidence of frequent demand in return for meager recompense; I could clearly see the physiognomies of the tourists, still miles away, and even more clearly the desire, flaring up obliquely in the eyes of the commentator, literally to act out the role of those whose role they were only acting

And who are you to feel superior? Didn't they put on a glorious gypsy show for you during your first visit, and didn't you sit there entranced in the shrill, smoky twilight of the *csárda*, dreaming into the last of the sunset (and to enjoy that kind of happiness you didn't even first have to lug suitcases

Against a red traffic light, a young man runs across the intersection to catch a moving streetcar, and the policeman on duty looks on with interest, wondering whether the young man will make it

Outside the bakeries, waiting for fresh bread on Saturday: the only line one ever sees. On Saturdays there is never enough bread, so Gábor explains; they seem to forget that Saturday is invariably followed by Sunday when, of course, no baking is done. The only kind of bread produced is wheat bread that stays fresh for days after being cut. It is sold in kilo or half-kilo chunks sliced off big round loaves, and pieces are selected as if they were filet steaks: No, not that one – that one there, if you don't mind, no no, I mean the one right at the back there – yes, and then that one way over on the right! Sometimes a housewife buys a whole loaf and carries it tucked under her arm the way they carry their children here. Then there is white bread in all sorts of smaller shapes: pretzel, snails, twists, braided, sugared, salted, with poppy seed, with caraway seed, but always white bread, very white, very firm, very rich, very bad for you. Theoretically, black bread is available, says Gábor, you just have to know where, but he doesn't know either, must be in some specialty store or other

Wherever you look, at every street corner, on every square that profusion of flowers! Not a block without its flower shop and, between shops, the stalls of flower sellers: pails of carnations, pails of gladioli, pails of marguerites, pails of asters, bowls of pansies, jars of violets, pitchers of African daisies, baskets of everlasting flowers, tubs of chrysanthemums, on the walls pussy willows, branches of chestnut and helleborus, vine leaves and oak leaves, reeds and twigs, and on damp cloths piles of roses of every color, the cheapest costing five forints each, the most expensive twenty; and in the evening the flower sellers walk through the restaurants with their baskets, and if you want to buy flowers at three o'clock in the morning you will always find a way. The word "gallant" still has a ring of freshness about it: men give flowers, flatter, pay compliments and kiss hands, and no flattery could be so sugary as to be unpalatable. Of course, this cult of women points to a robust male domination that is plainly reflected in the language:

when she marries, a woman loses not only her maiden name but also her given name: a Miss Rózsa Polgár (or, to follow Hungarian usage: a Miss Polgár Rózsa) who marries a Mr. Szabó János becomes not Mrs. Szabó Rózsa but Szabó Jánosné, "Tailor John wife." All she keeps is her nickname, and this has usually been given her by her fiancé: Riki, Tiki, Fifi, Tuti, Taki, Flocki, Mini, Lili, Zuzu, Szusu, Tsutsu, Kiki, Zsuzsu

At the secondhand bookstore (the one around the corner, the largest), among some twelve thousand volumes (including a thousand in German) for me only one: Molnár's *Liliom*

"Breakfast is included in the price of the room; an ineradicable compensation bequeathed by the Hapsburgs to their erstwhile dominion." This is how you had formulated it in your head, but as you are writing it down the thought occurs to you: How come "ineradicable"; why "compensation"; for what reason the "Hapsburg dominion" – why on earth this marshaling of pejoratives? Why are you so annoyed by this rule? You come up with a ready answer: because your freedom of movement is financially restricted and you are under compulsion to have your breakfast here! But that, my good friend, isn't true either. You're not even paying for it, P.E.N. is paying for it, and you could turn it down at no expense whatever and have your breakfast somewhere else! So there is no economic compulsion, but there is a temptation, and that's what you resent. You had decided to live entirely on fruit and albumen, and now, in addition to a hot or cold dish of your choice (small steak; scrambled eggs with sausages, ham and eggs, eggs in a glass, salami, ham, cold cuts, cold roast meat, cheese), you are faced with a glass of aromatic peach nectar, a little

24

dish of snowy whipped cream, a basket of large breakfast rolls, still warm, or (for regular guests) little golden-brown salted croissants – and all of this free of charge, and you're supposed to turn your back on it? You can't; and that's why you fall back on the Hapsburgs

What it boils down to is this: you have a privilege (a free breakfast), and you would rather it had no strings attached. And it is this hidden desire that causes your morality to run rampant

Did the Hapsburgs really introduce this practice, did they promote it, did they impose it on anyone? You don't know, but you formulate a denunciation

Formula of wishful thinking: S must not be P! But that is already the cultivated, intellectualized form; in its robust origins it would simply be: S must not be S! That's how children think, and that's how shamans act

But there was another, no less important (really no less?) reason for your formula. You had been looking for something to express the following: the continuing influence of specific traits of urban life-style and hospitality in the present territory of the former Hapsburg empire. A simple example instead of a laborious description: "Eggs in a glass" is known in every town and village between Vienna, Prague, Budapest, and Lvov, but, except in first-class establishments, not in Saxony, Brandenburg or Silesia. How are we to define this common characteristic? "Imperial Hapsburg"? That's much too negative. "Austrian"? That denies the multinational origin. "Southeastern European"? That would imply that Southeastern Europe started to the northwest of Bavaria and ended at the Greek-

Albanian-Bulgarian-Romanian border. "Balkan" or "Levantine" would be completely off-base. How, then? "In the Hapsburgs' erstwhile dominion." Why not, and what's wrong with that? And what is the linking of breakfast to the room price if not a compensation? Of course it is. And is it ineradicable? Since it has persisted, this also is probably true. So you were right after all with your original formula

Crappy way to earn a living

Bent on acquiring the status of a regular patron I place a few forints on the table for a tip as I leave, and note with disapproval that everybody else has the same idea

Breakfast coffee, incidentally, is always made with chicory, and anyone who doesn't know this and is thinking of the legendary *dupla* as he orders, makes a face at the first sip. You can count on it – futurology. But why you are served chicory for breakfast no one knows, not even Zoltán, and he knows all there is to know about Hungary

Clear day, blue sky, wind over the Danube. So: walk around the city, across to Buda, up Gellért Hill, uphill, downhill, around the castle as far as St. Margaret's Island, and around the Great Ring onto Rákóczi Street back to the hotel

Down to the Danube: again, and I recall for the first time without distress, that Hungarian officer who, one night in the Caucasus, while we were being deloused, yelled at me as we stood by the wooden tub steaming over the fire: "You blew up our bridges, all the bridges of Budapest, you've destroyed the beauty of Hungary," and I yelled back: "But that was to stop the Russians coming!" and he yelled: "They came anyway!" and I yelled: "Because not nearly enough was blown up!" How this argument arose, I can't remember; all I can see is the Hungarian's face, chalk-white in the firelit gloom, and know that I then ran out in a rage, naked, as far as the barbed wire between the oak trees, thinking of the culture of the West, which apparently did not include bridges

The ecstasy in the voice of that Hungarian, which even his hatred could not disguise: the bridges of Budapest, the beauty of Hungary. ... I couldn't share his emotion, never having seen Budapest, and even if I had I was a Fascist and wallowed in a spirit of defiance which I considered extremely heroic; counterpart of a *quia absurdum*

Fourteen years later, during my first visit, as I was gazing rapturously on the city from Freedom Hill, György said: "What you're looking at is a beauty without a nose, St. Elizabeth Bridge is still missing, haven't you noticed the horrible gap?" I nodded, for I had noticed and yet I hadn't, since to me it did not look horrible, and György repeated softly: "A queen without a nose

Do contradictions exist in reality, or are they created by the depiction of reality? Depict a body on a flat surface, and a contradiction is created – i.e., that something three-dimensional is two-dimensional

(My friend the mathematician likes to scoff; a contradiction occurs when Thesis A applies on Mondays, Wednesdays and Fridays, its negation on Tuesdays, Thursdays and Saturdays, and on Sundays neither of them

O bridges of Budapest: Petőfi-híd; Szabadság-híd; Erzsé-bet-híd; Lánchíd; Margit-híd; Árpád-híd – Petőfi Bridge, Freedom Bridge, St. Elizabeth Bridge, Chain Bridge, St. Margaret Bridge, Árpád Bridge: I have long been searching for an image to capture you, and this time again it will elude me. Two cities, and in two respects as utterly different as low plain and mountain range, *and* metropolis and dream city: Buda in the hills around the castle, Rome and Rose Hill; Pest roaring away in smoke and neon lights around its Western and Eastern Stations. ... The Danube divides yet unites; reflected in it, the seemingly irreconcil-able is reconciled, only in it do Buda and Pest become Budapest. The river unites, and its waters separate what it has united; the bridges fasten the two halves of the city together while pushing them apart; the magnificent curves of the suspension bridges lead the hills down into the plain, and the plain uses the long backbones of the bridges to thrust into the hills and at one point all the way through the rock. ... Outstretched arms in loose sleeves, that might be the beginnings of an image, but then the arms must give the effect of ribs within a body

Where Pannonia and *puszta* meet head on, fire would break out were it not for the cooling powers of the river: instead, the city was formed

And what a sap you are, racking your brain over the reality of contradictions while standing right in the middle of one:

$$BUDA + PEST = BUDAPEST$$

But then you should recognize the essence of Pest in Buda too, and of Buda in Pest, and that is exactly the case: self-recognition in the opposite

And the depiction? It wipes out the contradiction

The Hegelian formula one can never tire of contemplating: if p turns into q, then q also turns into p

"I don't really know the Danube, I've never seen it in a rage!" But you did see it in its calm; haven't you enough imagination to see it in its fury? Have you enough imagination to see the insect when you see the chrysalis? So does the surface deceive? It points to the depths

At my hosts' to discuss my program: I can do what I like, travel (free of charge) wherever I like, visit whoever and whatever I like, work when I like, be as lazy as I like, my sole commitment being an evening of readings

Discussion with Ferenc about the Caucasus anecdote; his first reaction: these present years offer the last chance, otherwise a crucial characteristic of our era – that period of change in the POW camp – would remain virtually unwritten, for only our own generation could do this job, and if it didn't get to work on it soon – no, immediately – that piece of history would be lost forever to sensory consciousness. ... He gets all worked up; I shrug my shoulders and say "Oh well," and know he is right, have known it for twenty years, and never knew it with as much equanimity as now

Why does it seem so objectionable that the women here smoke wherever they happen to be – on the street, in phone booths, shopping, at table between the soup and the meat? Why do I find it indecent, almost repulsive? Is it an encroachment on a male prerogative? But then the Hungarian males would be the first to resist, yet they don't. Does it give them an alibi for regarding women as equals? True, the men smoke just as much, cigarettes are dirt-cheap, but with the men one puts up with it. Interesting test: does it seem equally objectionable in old women? Funny: they don't smoke

St. Elizabeth Bridge, incredibly slender, not an ounce of fat, all function

Cheap, that's the right word. The continuous puffing looks cheap. Does this mean that the person making himself cheap in this way is dear to you, or you want him to look dearer

Outside the parish church three gypsy children are begging, indescribably dirty, indescribably cheerful, the oldest perhaps seven, the others five. At the sight of me, they surround me with outstretched hands. A woman walking to church on the other side of the street escorted by several men, calls out to me sternly: "Don't give them anything! Don't give them a thing!" and, seeing that I am not to be deterred and don't chase the children away, she thumps her umbrella on the ground: "Can't you hear me? You're not supposed to give them anything!" I give each of them a forint, the smallest one beams but the taller one says solemnly: "I'm the oldest, you must give me two forints!" I give; they clap their hands and laugh out loud, and the little one hops around like a bear, proudly displaying her coin and chanting: "I've got a forint, I've got a forint!" Two middle-aged women stop for a moment, wistfully stroke the children's heads, nod sorrowfully, and give nothing. The children laugh. I have stepped into the porch to continue watching them. They notice my interest and rush at me with shrill cries. The oldest girl lifts her ankle-length skirt as she runs; I take refuge in the church, and through the open window see Saint Gellért on his black hill ominously brandishing his crucifix

The gypsy children have disappeared, and the river bank with its strolling crowds is now depopulated

What do we really mean by cheap? "At the lower level of the price range"; "decidedly below the value." The distinction between price and value originates with political economy. Value expresses the economic nature of an article, price the surface of this nature. Hence "cheap" indicates both, and how sensitive we are to such differences in the one word: "The puffing is cheap" – "This room is cheap

While on this word: the more we penetrate its essence, the more one moral factor suppresses the other, previously determining factors. Look for similar words

In a pastry shop I try to order something in Hungarian and unwittingly say something highly objectionable and feel completely at a loss. In this respect Hungarian is tricky: confusing long with short vowels or voiced with unvoiced consonants often leads to fantastic misunderstandings. Last year when I was trying to buy some greenstuff in a village co-op and had spent hours memorizing the necessary phrase, I ended up asking the salesgirl whether she had a nice green ass, merely because, although the words otherwise sound alike, "ass" is pronounced short and "stuff" long. The girl, hardly seventeen, shrieked and fled, and her father appeared, and he weighed three hundred pounds

What makes this language seem so strange? Acoustically: by the agglomeration of syllables ending in "k" – "ak," "ek," "ik," "ok," "ünk." You have to concoct a ridiculous example to imitate this: "Pick up that pink rock, Jack, and sock it back to Dick." But that doesn't sound in the least Hungarian since it fails to reproduce the stressing of the length or brevity of a vowel; the short "o" pronunciation of the letter "a" (peculiar to this language) expelled throatily through half-open lips; the syncopated discrepancy between emphasis and length of two syllables, as for example in "Úngaarland"; and the heavy stress of the first syllable that dactylizes the entire intonation

Optically: the excessive length of many words; the clash of sibilants and the use of "c" with no mitigating "h" or "k"; the frequency of "y"; the superabundance of umlauts, especially the "ö"; the superabundance of stress accents and the stress accents even on umlauts; the superabundance of the word *a*, the definite article which we are tempted to misinterpret as the indefinite article

My hotel room once again facing the narrow lane, and across the way, outside four second-floor windows, just like last year, the defective shutters, half raised and aslant, with human torsos in sweaters and pants gliding past against subdued light

Dream:
I am walking with my father across a stony field; we walk all day and finally, on the verge of collapse, we come to a hotel. We are shown to a room, four bare walls, containing nothing but a chair and a tiny wardrobe. My father is about to protest, but I say: Look, Father, that's the way things are nowadays,

all you get anywhere is the basics; the basics of
money, basics of food, basics of freedom, and this
happens to be the basics of a hotel room. You need a
chair, you need a bit of a wardrobe, you don't really
need a table or a bed

October 17

Daily breakfast pleasure: the bilingual news sheet for foreigners put out by the Hungarian News Service – excellently produced, extremely fast and, in spite of its limited space, widely informative. The very layout is smart: German in front and English on the back, alternating weekly, to avoid any show of preference

This news sheet is aimed not at promotion but at being a news medium, i.e., at informing as well as entertaining, and in that way it does promote and makes an excellent job of it

I read that yesterday's sudden temperature drop from twenty-five to five degrees Centigrade claimed six victims in Hungary

Courtesy calls: how is it they never fail to wrap the spottiest and most wilted roses without my noticing? (And they are always the most expensive ones too

The narrow galleries encircling the inner courtyards. Encircling what? Emptiness, hollow space, nothing – a form of baroque

A natural wonder outside Ilona's house: how do you persuade three tomcats sitting in a row to swing their tails in time? You can't. If they were forced to, they wouldn't

The inner courtyards make you think of the human body, its exterior and interior – and of course this image is wrong! The human body is more like a building constructed around a utility shaft with a garbage chute in its invisible interior

(Later: in an old guidebook, I find this comparison:

"Why should my imagination not be allowed to think of Pesth as a beauteous reclining maiden, her feet curving backward and one arm outstretched beside her head while her left hand shyly attempts, like that of the Medici Venus, to cover the lower part of her torso. The lovely countenance [the New Town] smilingly admires its own reflection in the clear mirror of the Danube, and the two resplendent buildings, the Casino and the Theater, which, due to the unexpected beauty of their outlines, stand out from the massed symmetrical rows of buildings, might be considered the maiden's breasts. With equal aptness the crooked winding lanes of the Old Town indicate the intestines and thus the lower abdomen, a comparison borne out by the fact that the waterfront forming the extremities of the Old Town on the left bank of the Danube consists mostly of malodorous tanners' quarters. ..."

Ferenc: In our country an author can write anything he likes so long as it's not Fascist!

Sounds impressive, but is he correct? In a society that believes it has complete literary freedom, one would have to start systematically from its self-imposed taboos, from its own controls, its internal censorship. But then one is immediately struck by: consideration and a sense of shame, two factors that must not be regarded as purely moral, as wholly extra-literary factors. An indecent offense against the demands of consideration also jeopardizes anything previously written by the offender; and a certain measure of shame (not only, and certainly not primarily, sexual) seems to me an essential qualification for a writer.

Moreover, those modifying relationships between observer and observed, between subject and object, known to us from physics, psychology, medicine and other disciplines, apply also to literature: were a totally shameless mode of observation possible, it would probably cease to have any human object, and even its final creation would no longer be human. But I still find all this terribly confusing, even the terminology; I just feel that there are some strong currents which must be resisted

Shamelessness, needless to say, is not identical with blatancy or exhibitionism, which usually produce feeble literature. A book of profoundly moving shamelessness is Saint Augustine's *Confessions*

And of course it is quite ridiculous to assume a direct reciprocity or a direct ratio between the moral (pedagogic, political, cultural-pedagogic, even ethical and cultural) and the aesthetic in the sense of "the more – the more", for instance: the more chaste the more aesthetically valuable; the more obscene the more aesthetically valueless. ... The cultural pedagogue may have his justification, but I have mine too and insist upon it when I use those terms free of value

Can shame find expression in form, in the formal? A form can of itself be offensive, at least in Germany, that we know. But then there should also be shame – and I don't mean in the sense of shame at unsuccessful forms, I mean form as an expression of shame, a shame-form

The massive use of quotation marks in the wrong place, for example, is a formal expression of inner insecurity

A society without taboos would be inhuman. It could not even materialize. And what are you emphasizing here? I would hope: the inhuman

"The opposite of an error is again an error" – a favorite saying of Johannes R. Becher; suddenly I grasp what lies behind it

On Kossuth Street, almost side by side: night-club display, with photos of the variety turns, and display of a Christian devotional-supply store, and on the faces of the dancer kneeling in adoration and of the saint kneeling in adoration the same expression of contrived ecstasy, betokening the same physical stupidity

Imagine such displays for everything that is advertised but not embodied in material goods: displays for foreign policy, for national welfare, for youthful exuberance, for cultural policy

That evening, Molnár's Líliom, and all my longings are reawakened. ... Unforgettable words: "Any roofer can repair a roof! To be a barker in the city park is far more difficult!" – "People think that when they die there's' nothing more to worry about!" – "I sit beside the cash register and read the papers and supervise the waiters and all that big-city bustle!" This is said by the owner of a suburban bistro; and is intended to convey grotesque megalomania; however, if the suburban bistro is part of the big city, the big city must necessarily be mirrored in it, and if it does not seem to do so we should not scold either of them but try to see more acutely

In Berlin, look up Schiller's "Pleasure in Tragic Subjects"; finally get hold of Chesterton's "A Defense of Penny

Dreadfuls," etc.; collect material for "A Defense of Revelry"; reflect for the hundredth time on kitsch

Is pleasure in the pleasures of the lower middle class, lower-middle-class? If so, only if it happens on a lower-middle-class level, i.e., sneeringly or pharisaically. The yearning for poetry, even where satisfied by the bogus, is always a great human trait and can unquestionably be the object of great poetry. Little Mary Smith, sobbing over her pulp novel, seems to me more likeable than the philistine poetry-administrator who, while condemning her, does not even do that

Self-censorship is dependence on language: my drawer contains fragments which, out of consideration for someone close to me, I do not complete. If for every degree of relationship the language had only the one, undifferentiated word "relation," I could publish them, and the factual accuracy would not suffer, for in that case the word "relation" would include that specific relationship which represents the point of my contemplated work, a relationship which today no one thinks of in the normal usage of the word "relation." However, if there existed only that one collective term without differentiation, I would probably no longer feel that incident to be worth recording

Or hyperdifferentiation: the Hungarian language contains separate words for "younger sister", "older sister" – there you could simply reverse reality. But aren't you deceiving yourself again – wouldn't this linguistic distinction be rooted in such basic differences in reality that by turning the older person into the younger, or vice versa, your story would in turn become inaccurate

Liliom: the hatred between vagabond and policeman almost a fact of life. Do such hate-relationships have an elemental origin, like the hatred with which railwaymen pursue a tramp in Jack London's America, a hatred that can find satisfaction only in killing the Other? Or that hatred for everything creative in which a certain type of sterile human being seeks satisfaction

Is the impetus of such hatred always envy

Carping rule of the German *Duden* dictionary that sometimes overshoots the mark, or rather: strives for the irrational goal of total regimentation, never to capitalize the German word for "other" (*andere*), i.e., never to treat it as a noun since it can always be augmented by a noun (in this case: killing "the other person"). But what happens when I want to emphasize what separates rather than what is common? And what, for heaven's sake, when someone is only the Other, nothing but the Other, in a dialogue for instance: The One – the Other? Or when the Other is not simply of another species subordinate to a common overall concept, but rather the Other that is incommensurable to what is mine? Answer given by a German when asked why he had studied Romance languages: "It was the desire for the completely Other!" Or in Füst: "the dark Other" – not "other person," not "other spirit," but: Other

"He has wrestled a thousand times with the Other, who may not be alive but whose victory over him is certain. Not because he might have better qualities, but because he is the Other. ..."

These words were written by Karl Kraus, who capitalized the German word for "other," and Karl Kraus knew his German all right

"Watch out, watch out, O vagabond/The gendarme has his eye on you" – this song, of Líliom's also applies to writers: *Duden*'s lexicographers are on the *qui vive*

Noise, laughter and singing below: young people marching along the street, led by a band made up of saucepans and washboards and rolling pins

From the next room a waltz is burrowing through the wall. No, not burrowing, seeping

In the morning, before waking, this dream:
**Entering a huge room with Ursula, a completely
empty windowless room with whitewashed walls
that in some sinister way seems familiar to me. We
have entered through a door in the rear wall and
stand hesitantly just inside as our eyes scan the
room: not a trace of use, not a trace of wear, and
yet not new. Long, awkward silence, finally I say:
You know what? I think my parents used to live
here! Ursula shakes her head, and even I don't
really believe what I say, but I boldly step forward
into the room, stretching out my groping hands,
although it's not dark: I touch cobwebs. Watch out,
a trap! says Ursula. Nonsense, I say, look, there are
cobwebs here, that means no one's been here for ages,
we needn't be afraid to go in! Ursula silently shakes
her head again, but I go farther into the room, and
nothing happens. Suddenly ahead of me, against the
whitewashed wall, I see a white kitchen stove, its
top and doors and ashbox are white too.
I step closer and grasp the handle of the oven door:
it is cold, the top of the stove is cold too,
and I think: There you are — not used! I open
the door and inside I see a second stove, also all white,
and I open this one too, but its door is not quite so cold.
As I feel this I am seized with fear, but I open
the second door too, and inside the second stove
I see a third one, also white, but instead of a flat
top there is a grill, with glowing coals under it,
and on the grill a pot with a heaving brew containing
floating pieces of grayish-white meat and fat.
Human flesh, I know at once, and swing around in**

**horror to find myself alone in the room and the only
door silently closing**

Newspaper item: 'Flu is invading Hungary

The dream is linked with the episode at the railway station
(opening the trunk; black car, two black suitcases, with the
usual inversion of black into white. Elga's comment:
Otherwise he's lost

Unpacked grammar and textbook after all. Not likely to
remember any new words, such is the bitter experience of
serious efforts; but I might be able to take a few small
steps nearer the spirit of the grammar, the spirit of the
language: e.g., what is the significance of the word order,
which is sometimes diametrically opposed to our own?
Needless to say, this word order is just as "normal" as the
one we are familiar with, there being no such things as
"normal" or "abnormal" languages, but a better grasp of
the logic of this word order would lead to a better grasp
of the soul of the speakers

(A plausible explanation would be: first things first, e.g.:
"Lakatos Ferenc dr. phil. úr" rather than the German "Herr
Dr. phil. Ferenc Lakatos." "1926. május 5." rather than:
"May 5, 1926," or the British "5 May 1926." Even the full
stop in the Hungarian date conveys a lot

(Analogously, the suffixes and postpositions: "Buda-
pesten" – "in Budapest"; "Berlinnél" – "near Berlin

And why do the numerals require no plural? Hungarians
say: two bread, three flower, hundred man, even with the
(in Hungarian single-gender) article: the two bread, the

hundred man. This is not, as appears at first sight, an adjectival use of the numeral, in Hungarian the adjective is never declined; it indicates a phonetic equality between collective concept and single concept. When I ask what it would sound like if the numeral were linked with the plural, Ferenc says: "Funny, because quite superfluous, but also rather beautiful in an archaic sort of way!" And he adds: "The plural is already implied in the numeral, so why go to double trouble!" "You mean: (That is) two (times one) bread, hundred (times one) man?" "Don't try to oversimplify," says Jutta, "or you'll never learn it! There are no analogies; you have to accept that Hungarian is different!" Very well, but what is the spirit of this difference? Once you get hold of that you will be able to formulate it. And when will you get hold of it? When you master the language. As usual, there is no other way! What I am doing now is comparable to someone opening a book on mathematics for the first time and being elated at the discovery of the dominant influence of Christianity on algebra because he sees addition expressed by a crucifix

The Metro: a hundred and thirty feet down into the depths, by escalator of course, only by escalator, an endless grinding journey, so it seems, and I feel dizzy when I look down. The abyss draws you down; that lovely autumn poem by Gábor ends with the line: "Be on your guard: withered leaves: they draw you down!"

I happen to think of my correspondence on the problems of writing and the complaint of my correspondent about the disappearance of the model that had prevailed in literature, including bourgeois literature, and which was destroyed by the introduction of such categories as inner conflict and change. Assuming this to be true, and apart from the fact that attempts to carry on the tradition of the immutably established model have been, and continue to be, for the most part unsuccessful: the breakdown of this static model was evidently the price for the emergence of a superior typification – one of movements, trends, processes, in terms both of the individual and society. Such types even produce concrete genres, like the novella or, in our day, the short story

The question of the next-highest degree goes beyond the potential of human experience: types of movement of movements, that's where religions offer their answers and the teleologies come to the surface

It seems I didn't quite understand my correspondent. The movements I was just talking about are as old as the hills: they are the mythologems, the generalizations of human experience on the road from primitive existence to oneself, the basic elements and primeval design of all poetry

On the Metro escalator, going up as we go down, children squatting, lovers face to face, people reading, chatting, others being borne anxiously toward that tricky step leading to *terra firma*; people frustrated in their hurry, tired people; indifferent, expectant, weary, impatient people; people savoring their respite: material for an unwritten, never-to-be-written literature, and gone forever, and ceaselessly reproduced – hence no reason whatever for sentimentality

Test: what is the first number you think of at the sight of these hordes of strangers? Strict requirements: they must be separated from you by a barrier, there must be no body contact, there must be no sharing in a common destiny, they must be observable with Kantian disinterest

The Metro cars so beautifully clean and comfortable that only the grubby dare sit down

The fact that the doors not only close but open automatically is more than a convenience: it also prevents many an irritation, however rudimentary, over one's fellowmen

Hungaria, the most famous of all famous coffee houses in Budapest, is still closed "for renovations." One wonders how Hungarian literature can continue to be created

Secondhand bookstore: vast quantities of dog-eared crime stories, vast quantities of dog-eared dime novels, vast quantities of dog-eared magazines, and somewhere among all these – how we searched for this back home! – one of Karl Kraus's Shakespeare adaptations, *Timon of Athens*

Imagine the reverse: if among stacks of literary and political periodicals you were to discover to your delight a vintage crime story from the "Super Thriller" series

Framed in the tall, snow-white rectangular superstructure of St. Elizabeth Bridge stands Saint Gellért, like an object in the viewfinder of a camera. A black figure, black in his semicircle of white columns in the black rock, brandishing his crucifix as if about to hurl it down onto the intransigent city which, despite its innumerable churches, is at heart as heathen as ever

St. Elizabeth Bridge: a white-robed maiden's arms reaching out tenderly, irresistibly, toward the man of wrath, and when he parries with uplifted crucifix the parish church spires gently and humbly proffer, as with raised hands, two golden crosses, a benedictory Peace-be-with-you

Gellért: My Lord saith: I came not to send peace, but a sword

The crosses sparkle

On the banks of the Danube in Buda: halfway up the hill, a wide white semicircle of columns, a theatrical backdrop against which the saint poses in his bishop's vestments before a supplicating female. Well below in the bare rock, a welter of rumps and torsos: from belt to ankles, a man rising with gigantic genitalia; across from him, from pelvis to forehead a torso with lacerated abdomen: Prometheus, whose agony coalesces with the rock as in Kafka's parable, and down below, on the columns, sprayed by the waterfall, crouch the hissing eagles

Gellért green-flecked against the sky, the fulminating prophet: major theme of modern Hungarian literature, in Radnóti, in Füst. ... A comparison with contemporary German poetry (George, Rilke) would be worth-while

What enrages the prophet, against whom is he fulminating? Radnóti deals with the object of rage, Rilke takes rage as his subject and describes the How: George speaks from the pose of rage, from Füst rage speaks through the pose. Radnóti is full of rage, George is rage-filled, Füst rage itself, Rilke seeks to concentrate himself as the other extreme of rage, as humility. But of course none of these are value judgments

> "... rage keeps
> You alive; akin is the fire of
> Prophets and poets:
> Meat and drink for the people!"
> (Radnóti, 8th Eclogue

I gaze into Hungarian poetry like a deaf Ali Baba for whom, since he is past learning the magic opening formula, little windows have been cut into the Sesame mountain, one here, and one there, and another over there, and through these little windows he sees treasures sparkling, but never more than those afforded him by the windows, never the treasure as a whole, never in context. What he sees he can describe (translate into his own words), but he sees very little, only the magic spell can open up the mountain for him, but to learn this spell is denied him for evermore

Gellért smiles: *he* has learned Hungarian

The thin thread of the waterfall in the lofty baroque framework within the spacious framework of the little capitals along the way

In the rock, El Greco figures

In the rock, a giant ear

In the rock, a child

Sentence meted out, increased in severity by animals: reversion of humanity to a pre-totem era; the cruelest and most cynical humiliation, yet in a peculiar way a testimony to the humane: the executioner could, the culture cannot, show mercy, at most it could occasionally scorn, thus rendering torture and humiliation complete

In the Middle Ages, the hawk punishment: a victim strewn with raw meat, castrated by a bird of prey

Object of all these horrors: to deny humanity to the adversary by subordinating him to the animal or, better still, by forcing the delinquent to deny his own humanity, but in fact it is only the punisher who forfeits his own humanity. ... Béla the Great Christian had a sorceress imprisoned for so long that starvation drove her to devour her own feet, yet the chronicler is horrified not by the King but by this bestial woman

Shifting the burden of guilt: it was the animal that killed, for it could have refrained

In the final analysis: the alibi of divine consent, hence also the possibility of a common interest between victim and executioner. This is a criterion of any world that perceives itself as sound

Granted this world was consistent in minor details and toward minor victims: if the rope broke, the condemned man went free

The idea of divine ordeals horrifies us. That the decision as to true or false, guilt or innocence, life or death, was made contingent upon physical advantages or handicaps seems monstrous to us, and one wonders what happened to human common sense. Yet it was certainly present: physical inequality was the prerequisite for a miracle to occur, and a miracle was the essence of a divine judgment (in the case of equality, the miracle occurred in the form of a coincidence). To me this seems far more logical, in that kind of society, than the present-day requirement that a person – under extreme psychological and often physical stress, moreover – should be able at a given moment to "find the right word," "show remorse," "give a satisfactory explanation," "acknowledge his errors." "defend himself convincingly" – i.e., in each case attain an exceptional mental achievement which then will decide, although rarely over life and death, on vital aspects of his future existence

The eagles on the two pillars at the foot of Gellért Hill are holding snakes in their talons and these snakes are trying to sink their fangs into the enemy's flesh, but the eagles face each other with wide-open beaks and, as far as the reptiles below are concerned, are relying entirely on their capable claws

As usual, the chronicler tells his tale without comment; he records whatever he considers unusual, and that might just as well be the behavior of the King as that of the sorceress. Knowing what we do about this aspect of the climate of the times we must assume that to him the King's behavior seems normal and that of the prisoner abnormal. Thus by the mere act of telling he has taken sides against the victim, and his contemporaries and, much later, the great majority of Christianity will have interpreted him accordingly. Of course there are some people who condemn him for it. They overlook the fact that, with his uncommented report, this same chronicler has also enabled us to re-evaluate, that is to say, to condemn the King, a possibility of which the chronicler's critics take advantage. ... Later rulers were smarter and prevented such objectivity, and probably the worst perversion turned out to be Eichmann's movie about the happy life of the Jews in Theresienstadt

Radnóti saw it:
> "... he who moves today will vanish
> Into the void. ..."

Could a commentary by the chronicler have changed anything in the response to this account, could he have cast moral doubt upon the action of the King? Hardly, and the question is idle. It was not the chronicler's task to change anything; his job was to record the remarkable, and this he did: he reported that, under the rule of a Christian king, a woman was imprisoned under conditions such that starvation caused her to devour her own feet. No more, but also no less, and that is enough. "By all means take on the task of a partial function, but see that you fulfill it meticulously. ..."

And Theodor Haecker's memorable remark that he who confuses causes less harm than he who suppresses, for what has been confused can be restored to order, whereas what is incomplete will always remain outside of the original order

At the feet of Saint Gellért, looking across to Pest: the two crosses sparkle triumphantly, and beyond them the smoky city laughs triumphantly

The cars on the bridge move so slowly, they glide as if being pushed: a blue car, a purple one, a tan, a yellow, and of course black and green ones too; and alongside them, yellow and slow, the streetcar

Unthinkable for a Budapest to exist without these bridges; unthinkable for an empty space to gape here: Taglioni without a nose

This bridge is a romantic ballet, gossamer, a miracle of lightness, victory over matter. The trusses are threads of moonlight, the supports a filagree, its shadow a glitter

Finding an image for the bridges in their entirety is beyond me, I am afraid.

The separate images come crowding in on me:

Chain Bridge: Hun-black knight in clanking armor, lions crouching at his feet

Freedom Bridge: horizontal Eiffel Tower

St. Margaret Bridge: gate of the seven magic rivers

Petőfi Bridge: central part of a linear equation

Árpád Bridge is not visible from here (and an addition from later notes: killing three birds with one stone

A gypsy girl strolling along the quay is holding a little whip with two strands, at the end of each dangles a red ball the size of a walnut. The balls click as they collide, at first irregularly, lost in the noises all around, then suddenly in a very fast, staccato rattle like a machine gun, and the sparrows scatter clamorously from the tops of the chestnut trees

That evening a concert at the Academy of Music: Mozart, Ravel, Sárközy, concerto grosso, the second movement a nightmare, 1943. The audience largely conservative, demonstrating its rejection of untraditional music with folded arms

Outside the illuminated sign is out of order; instead of ZENEAKADÉMIA (Academy of Music) all you can read is ADÉMIA, the very word for a pop song, or neon tube poetry; start a collection

Spent the evening on Rose Hill in a small group of young people speaking Russian: that conversation, as welcome as all other expressions of internationalism, touches on an ever-open wound: with all the chances I have had, I might now be speaking seven languages! How I have wasted my youth, and here I've certainly no one to blame but myself

Of the utmost importance would be an accurate, down-to-earth analysis of our own Socialist counter-design for Europe: its foundation, its characteristics, its strengths and its defects, its possibilities and its perspectives (the real as well as the visionary

Outside, the night smells of buffaloes and smoke

Night view of Buda:
Part of the Milky Way simmering
Night view of Buda:
A sack of diamonds
Night view of Buda:
Convocation of the stars
Night view of Buda:
The bull snorting silver
Night view of Buda:
The nest of the Roc bird
Night view of Buda:
The moon goddess gives birth
Night view of Buda:
The shepherds keep watch
Night view of Buda:
A geode of light
Night view of Buda:
Seni's rapture
Night view of Buda:
Sidereal banquet
Night view of Buda:
The dark catches fire
Night view of Buda:

Danaë is waiting
Night view of Buda:
The girdle of Venus
Night view of Buda:
A surge of buoys
Night view of Buda:
Comforting the orphan
Night view of Buda:
Mine shaft of dreams
Night view of Buda:
Aladdin rubs the lamp
Night view of Buda and nostalgia
Besets you

night view of Buda, and Ilona will promptly come up to
you and say: "If you need to go, the washroom's over there
to the left

The taxi taking us back to our hotel is driven by a frail,
rather defenseless-looking woman. How does she cope
with the drunk customer who gets fresh? I ask Zoltán to
put it to her; he does, and with a laugh she waves away
the question: "Oh, I can take care of myself!" Almost half
of all taxis, says Zoltán, are driven by women, usually, as
now, on the basis of an increasingly popular arrangement:
the taxi is leased from the firm at a fixed monthly rate and
after a given time, usually ten years, becomes the property
of the lessee, who is free from the outset to use the vehicle
as he wants and pays the rent regardless of the turnover.
In view of our own dearth of taxis, this system seems to me
at least worth considering

As I fall asleep: a fly, making its weary way up toward
the light, dragging its long shadow in its wake

An amusing dream, but the moment I reach the door to turn on the light I have forgotten it. I can only remember that I was giving someone a hearty thrashing as I sang at the top of my voice, and that a bright blue moon was shining down

October 19

Budapest: perhaps even more mini-skirts than in Berlin, in any case shorter ones, sometimes ending above the top of the stocking, usually cheap materials with an inverted pleat back and front and the skimpiest ones covering the ungainliest thighs

The intersection outside the Astoria is a No Stopping zone, a taxi stops, the customer has trouble with his money, the driver explains, the customer searches, cars block the intersection, the cars blow their horns, the cars make a racket, the customer negotiates, the driver shows the figure on his fingers, the cars are now jammed up beyond the intersection, the customer doesn't understand, the cars roar, the driver of the car behind the taxi jumps out, cursing as he thumps the rear end of the taxi, the driver waves him off, the curser flings up his arms, and the cars way at the back reverse or turn and look for another route

Leaning against the wall in the gateway next to the bistro, eyes closed: What flows by? Hungarian, Viennese, Dutch, Hungarian, English, Viennese, Saxonian, Viennese, Hungarian, Hungarian, Saxonian, Italian, English, Saxonian, English, Slovakian, Styrian, Bavarian, some Slavic language, Hungarian, Hungarian, Hungarian, Swiss German, Hungarian, English, French, maybe Arabic or Hebrew, Saxonian, Viennese, Semitic again, Slavic again, Bavarian, Russian, Hungarian, Swiss German, Polish, Polish, Viennese, Czech, English, Slovakian, Hungarian, Swabian, Saxonian, Saxonian, High German, Hungarian, Styrian, unknown, English, Hungarian, English, English, Hungarian, English, French, and the French pauses beside me and addresses me, and it is György and Professor M. from

Strasbourg, who is doing some work on Radnóti and unfortunately has to return home this evening

Lunch with György and M. in a nearby bistro, two blocks away toward Joseph Town, and there, Gábor, they serve *bableves*, bean soup, and a gypsy roast, both very spicy and both hot, and both served in such a way that one is happy to concede the waiter's tribute, exacted by inclusion on the bill of a salad that was not served (the same thing, by the way, happened to me yesterday in Buda, and will no doubt happen again

Radnóti's grandiose example of a modern application of classic and, above all, ancient forms. In Germany such attempts in this century have almost always led to a sterile neo-classicism, a pretentious artiness (Weinheber) or a crypto-form of form-disintegration (Hauptmann's *Till Eulenspiegel*). The only real promise, so far as I know, is to be found in Hermlin, but he never expanded it

In his second eclogue, a conversation between poet and bombardier, Radnóti developed a new form of distich: an alexandrine with alternating four and three stresses in the first half-line; and although he wrote resignedly: "No one will notice it," this analytical "noticing" actually constitutes a second level of response. Preceding the prosodic perception is the almost physical impact upon the reader, and without the use of that new form this poem could not have exerted the cruel grip on the reader which now compels him to read the poem to the end

The grandiose state of transition in Radnóti: not only does the man merge with the machine, the machine also merges with the man, and to the degree that the bombardier mechanizes himself the murder apparatus humanizes itself and becomes a living companion. What even Radnóti could not foresee, of course, was the new nature of automated genocide, the perpetrator piloting from a desk

There are inklings, to be sure:

> "To him who flies on high the land is like a map,
> he cannot tell where Vörösmarty must have lived.
> ...
> What seems a target from above, a railway or a
> power plant,
> is but a signal box, the signalman in front,
> his flag aslant."

But at least those bombardiers still saw the land as an ordnance map, whereas for the bombers of Vietnam the ordnance map alone is land. This reversal is a mutation

Just as with the hawk punishment: separation of deed and perpetrator, of crime and criminal

In Radnóti this separation has not yet come about, hence his bombardier is a kind of Flying Dutchman of the skies, a technologized Ahasuerus. His bombardier still has sleepless nights; today's murderers sleep soundly

Another thing Radnóti could not foresee: the murder of the earth. In Vietnam the earth is being murdered, the land, the very matrix of life

This agonizing narrowing down of the question, what am I to do? to: what can I do

The almost total disappearance of political poetry is a phenomenon that should cause concern. Granted that other forms have emerged, the song of protest, for instance, but that is not a complete substitute. One of the reasons must be that I know no more about Vietnam than the newspaper does and that therefore I can say no more about it than the newspaper does. Nothing worse, because nothing does less service to a good cause, than a rhyming editorial

To see the newspaper page as the land – that is the very thing one must avoid. What's left? To describe one's own experiences of the destruction of man and earth

Once again: "By all means take on the task of a partial function, but see that you fulfill it meticulously. ..."
    Literature as a totem society: the writer at one with his subject, like the individual at one with his clan

I am against any law to regulate aesthetic practices and problems, but there is one law I would approve of: a ban on publishing any poems in free verse unless their author has previously produced convincing sample in strict form (rhymed, too, of course

While I am spelling out the theater programs on the side-walk poster pillar, I suddenly feel something warm nuzzling my feet: two gypsy children are shining my shoes, but the next instant along come the flower sellers flapping their rags as, scolding and threatening, they flail the air in the wake of the scattering children, and one of the women shouts words I don't understand but which, to judge by the scowls and gestures of their utterer, I can only interpret as the direst of threats

Took a bath: washed my shirts; since of course I cannot

hang my dripping nylon shirts in the wardrobe, I wrung
them out and remembered too late that that's a mistake. ...
Outside rain, dusk, in the next room the sound of a radio,
in the wardrobe a rhythmic dripping, and while studying
the lesson on *ik* verbs (the ones which when declined do
not disclose their root) I fall asleep

October 20

A cold; fever; leaden limbs: it's the 'flu! Can hardly get to my feet, but outside the weather is glorious, and I have four appointments to keep

At the pharmacy, to go with the pills, to make them slide down better, they sell you little squares of thin gelatine

There's that double string again with the clicking red balls

In the Vörösmarty pastry shop, the famous Gerbeaud, the secret focal point of Budapest. At the moment my brain is too fuzzy with 'flu, I'm too much under the weather, to be capable of sketching this aroma, this elegance: chandelier crystals reflecting crystal chandeliers; white-and-brown girls in brown-and-white uniforms serving chestnut ice cream with whipped cream; coffee in little cups with little lids; in the Elizabeth Room the Queen of Hungary used to partake of pistachio torte, and today the writers sit there in front of their daily twelve glasses of water, and Gábor introduces me to Iván Mándy, a big child with big eyes, and Gábor says to Mándy: "Listen he's written about old movie houses to," and Mándy's big blue eyes grow bigger and bluer, and Mándy says: "Naturally, what else is there to write about

Everything tastes of quinine and numbed feet

Mándy smiles even with his vest. ... I ask Gábor what else Mándy writes about, and Gábor says: "About football. About floozies. About hungry people. About melon eaters. About dreamers. About workers. About salesgirls. About children. About crazy city reporters. About cats —" and

Mándy, making a circle with his finger, summarizes the summary summarily: "Everything in the eighth district, but only the eighth

Antiquarian bookstore: barely a thousand books on the shelves, and those I would like to buy at first sight cost double my capital in forints

The lover of alliteration did the buying: Móricz; Mándy; Madách; Márk von Kált; Magyar Fairy Tales

But unfortunately no mythologies, no Kerényi, none of the out-of-print publications of the Hungarian Academy Press that I am looking for

Against mountains of grayish-yellow, bottle-shaped pears and oversize ruby-red apples, a basket of fresh figs: delicate pink, delicate gray, delicate brown, delicate purple; milky drops on the stalks (that is how, according to Ferenc's description, I imagine the poetry of Szabó Lőrinc

One day my obituary will contain the words: He carted around a lot of books and fruit

The market hall is overflowing with goods, but unfortunately something is lacking, olives and olive oil. Almost everywhere the customary self-service, in this case with deep plastic baskets; the cheese and sausage stalls are the only ones with the voucher system. I proceed according to the Russian method, add up the cost of the goods I want – two hundred grams of ham, two hundred grams of Emmental cheese – obtain a voucher from the cashier and attempt to exchange it for merchandise and get a mighty scolding: "What am I supposed to do with that scrap of paper, what do you expect me to do with it? Can't you have it weighed first and then pay? How am I supposed to slice exactly to the gram, two hundred grams to the last gram, it's unbelievable!" And she saws off (of course she is of enormous girth, of course she plants her left arm on her hip, of course she brandishes a butcher's knife, of course the girls come across from the next stall giggling, and of course a dignified elderly gentleman with a steel-gray mustache has faithfully and helpfully translated her scolding for my benefit), so she saws off a piece of Emmental, nearly a hundred grams too much, and I say: "That's fine, that's fine!" and pay for the rest

The saleswoman laughs; the elderly gentleman smiles; the young girls giggle and put their heads together and burst out laughing and run off with red faces

A good custom: at the meat stall you can also buy bread and rolls; this is pointed out to you if you don't

The attribute "Russian" threatens – from the most respectable motives –to be absorbed by the attribute "Soviet," with which it is by no means synonymous. "Soviet law," "Soviet diplomacy," "Soviet ethics," that makes sense; but "Soviet cognac" is pure nonsense since connoisseurs distinguish between Armenian and Georgian. Or "Soviet vodka," to denote the Russian variety, as distinct from the Polish. "Original Soviet cooking" is something I once read in Leipzig – with this wording the restaurant owner summarily wiped out a few hundred nationalities

Just manage to get home, fall into bed, swallow enough quinine (with gelatine) for five days, and call up Gábor,

Jutta, Ferenc and Zoltán to bring medicines for drastic treatment

An anthology by Corvina of Hungarian love poems (a contributor's copy of which I have unaccountably not received). Of special beauty a love poem by Nemes Nagy Ágnes, of whom I have hardly read anything: *Thirst*. It is the thirsting after an ecstatic fulfilment by actual devouring, destroying of the partner, but: "I love you; you love me ... hopeless!"

This poem has become part of my private treasure-hoard. And: a bow to the translator

High time, by the way, to emerge from the tombs

One of the translations in this volume provides bitter confirmation of my motto (on account of which I have been accused of arrogance): No translation at all is better than a bad one. Here is one of a poem by József; if I didn't happen to have a line-by-line translation in my suitcase, I would shrug my shoulders after the second verse and say: A very weak poem! And if I knew nothing of József's greatness, I would conclude: A very weak poet! In this case, though, antiquated words and phrases point so strongly to the translator that I would refrain from drawing any conclusion as to the original. The worst thing is the mediocrity that turns everything into the same mush

Be kind to the translator? Was he kind to the original author?

Rage and 'flu are locked in battle: shark versus octopus, and the octopus wins

Among my loot: G. Róbert Gragger, *Ancient Hungarian Stories*, and here at last I find something about the wrathful Gellért of whom I had only known that he was placed in a nail-studded barrel and rolled down into the Danube from that very mountain from which he now fulminates. This, then, is his life: Born in Venice; rich family; excellent education; father killed in a crusade; the son, by that time already an abbot, wishes to emulate the father and march against the heathen dogs in the Levant but instead, by Divine decree, marches against the heathen Hungarians, in preparation for which he prays, fasts and forgoes sleep for seven years in the desert of Beel. ... Confidant of King Stephen; tutor of princes; bishop; scholar of rank; after the apostasy of the Hungarians from Christianity, stoned, rolled into the Danube, and finally pierced by a lance, and "for seven years the river foamed at that spot yet did not wash away the blood. ..."

An endearing observation on the part of the old chronicler: "When he [Gellért] was writing one day and, due to excessive imagination, was overcome by sleep. ..."

An unexpected side of Gellért: "Whenever King Stephen was about to punish one of his begotten sons with the rod of justice for his misdeeds, Father Gellért would defend him with tears of compassion. ..."

And one episode which cannot be sufficiently thought about: Gellért is traveling with a company of knights when he suddenly hears a mill creaking and at the same time a woman singing. Coming closer he discovers a woman turning the mill as she sings, and he asks his companion: "Tell me, Walter, is the mill being moved by art or by labor?"

Walter, "By both, Father, by art and by labor, for it is

not being turned by some beast, rather must one's own hand turn with it!"

Gellért: "What a strange business, the way the human race feeds itself. Were there no art, who could endure the labor?"

A pronouncement I heartily endorse

Date of the martyr's death: 1047. The year when the witches appeared to Macbeth

Was Gellért really the zealot he is painted? I think not; no stout-hearted stalwart Saint Boniface, no hewer of oak trees, but probably a very shrewd diplomat. Furthermore, I read, he was "of small stature," and "all his powers were consumed utterly in the service of God."

One is tempted to reduce him to the formula: a highly cultivated reactionary, but such formulas say little, and this one is probably wrong at that. Anyone wanting at that time to turn the Magyars into a European nation had presumably to christianize them. Be that as it may: the fact that he has a monument and that it is illuminated at night really pleases me

Next door the radio is bellowing out one waltz after another. "Were there no art, who could endure the labor?"

But how to endure art

By labor

October 21

Fever. Groggy. Stupid. Bloated. And now, to top it all, heart pains from the quinine

Jutta, Gábor, Ferenc and Zoltán send medicines: Jutta multicolored capsules without instructions, Gábor white pellets with a double set of instructions, Ferenc quinine with gelatine, Zoltán apricot brandy, and Elga an invitation to the Lukács baths – today was her day for swimming and would I like to join her. I swallowed three capsules, three pellets, three doses of gelatine, bow reverentially and longingly to the *barackpálinka* and accept Elga's invitation

Heaven sends a warning signal: the taxi driver has never heard of the Lukács baths but instead recommends the Rudas, extols the Király baths, instead of turning right beyond St. Elizabeth Bridge is about to turn left toward the Gellért baths and, since I insist on Lukács and also remember Frankel Leo Street where it is located, he finally puts me down at the neighboring Császár baths, the Emperor's baths. "Császár baths", he says, "you can see for yourself, only the Császár baths, just Császár, no Lukács; Császár baths here, Császár baths there and beyond that Császár baths and again Császár baths and then nothing

There where there is nothing is the entrance to the Lukács baths

Have I now deprived the Császár baths? Supposing that due to this shortfall they fail to fulfill their plan and their female attendants lose their bonus – would I be to blame

The ancient yellow plane trees in the courtyard inspire confidence. Dappled sunlight, shade and silence, broad leaves drifting down, votive tablets of fervent gratitude on the crumbling walls, and swinging past them on two chrome-plated crutches a slender young one-legged woman

A text meriting inclusion in anthologies of great examples: "As doctor and patient I give thanks for the miraculous healing water!"
Beside it, above it: Latin, Cyrillic, Gothic, Arabic script

Two swimming pools, one square, the other long and rectangular; hot water here, cooler water there. We are almost alone, a few elderly gentlemen, a few elderly ladies, sunshine and silence, I shiver in the air, but the water feels good

In the winter, when snowflakes were falling here, Flaubert's horrifying damnation and resurrection

The one-legged woman hops into the cold pool; she is even more slender and delicate than her dress revealed, perhaps also in contrast to the clumsy stump of flesh dangling from her right hip. From behind, utterly repulsive and pitiful (which is almost the same); from the front, where the incisions in the stump are visible, fantastically obscene

An old woman, supervised by an even older one, performs her daily swimming stint, and the older woman, smoking and polishing her nails on a towel, walks beside the old woman, keeping up a ceaseless flow of comment

The seven pool attendants yawn

A portly sixty-year-old, perhaps even fatter than I am, wearing blue-and-white striped knee-length cotton swim trunks, performs the ritual of entering the pool (cold). Seated on the shallow steps leading to the bottom of the pool, he scoops up water in his palms, splashes it over knees and thighs, observes with pleasure the way it trickles and drips and sparkles as it runs off, then sprinkles his chest and the bulge around his navel; then, supported on hands and feet, he rocks himself inch by inch into the depths, delight spreading over his brown face as he emits groans of pleasure; the dome of his belly is still above water as his chest submerges, now his shoulders go under, his neck, the back of his head, there go his ears and, with a nimble twist as he plunges in, he pushes off and swims slowly and blissfully out into the Sea of Azov toward the wilds of Maeonia

The Hungarian's relationship to water is entirely naïve, entirely elemental, as I have found over and over again. ... That driver last year who set out on our trip to Lake Balaton, the car trunk full of empty bottles to bring home water from unknown springs – how he tasted it, how he savored it with nose and tongue, how he held the bottle up to the light, how he chewed the water! Or at the hot springs, the pleasant hours of chitchat and gossip, sitting in the water, on proper stone seats and chairs, smoking in the water, nibbling candy in the water, playing chess in the water, drinking mineral water in the water, enthusing over bathing experiences in the water, totally at ease in the relaxation of their hot and sulphur-immersed bodies. ... That time in Hévíz, that wallowing in body-temperature mud, came close to being an orgy. ... Or the water sampling in the legends of how the land was seized:

"Now when Kusid, on reaching the middle of the land of

Hungary and the region of the Danube, saw that the countryside was beautiful, the soil good and fertile, the water of the river pure and the grass luscious; all this pleased him. Then he went to the lord of the land, Svatopluk, who ruled after Attila. He brought greetings from his people and announced the reasons for his coming. Now when Svatopluk heard this he rejoiced, believing that peasants had come to cultivate his land. So he dismissed the messenger graciously. Kusid, however, filled a little barrel with water from the Danube, put some grass in his satchel, and also took along some clods of the black earth, and thus returned to his people. There he narrated all that he had seen and heard and laid before them the little barrel of water, the grass and the clods. All this pleased them greatly. They also tasted what had been put before them and convinced themselves that the soil was excellent, the water sweet and that even the grass of the meadows was as lush as the messenger had told them.

"Árpád then filled his horn with the water from the Danube and before the assembled Hungarians, with this horn in front of him, prayed aloud for the grace of almighty God: That the Lord might give this land unto them forever. And when he ended his prayer all the Hungarians cried out three times: 'God, God, God!'"

At the monastery school we had to wear our swim trunks in the bathtubs in the individual cabins, and the friar in charge used to peek through the keyhole and wish we would take them off

Last year, here on the sun roof, day after day the endless discussions about morals and literature, about Homer and modern literature, about Lukács and Anna Seghers, Thomas Mann, Henry Miller, Camus, the new Russian names, semantics and game theory, József and Freud, Füst, Madách, Ady, Wittgenstein. Such discussions in a large circle don't appeal to me at all, but there I joined in, and during the arguments one could see mountains and clouds, and the water was close

Beautiful, sad, yellow foliage

Among the plane trees Saint Luke's benevolent gaze follows two fledgling doctors

As I enter the cold pool to finish off, Elga warns me and, in view of my condition, advises the following sequence: first warm, then warmer and finally hot and then out, that was the way, then even the cold air couldn't hurt; but to cool off systematically meant catching your death

Into the steam bath – what a Minos palace! Coming from the swimming area, you walk up a few steps from the courtyard, pass through a corridor and, beyond a hall where perspiring old men sit in coats and hats, through a door marked EXIT you enter a tiled passageway traversed by sheeted figures and leading nightmarishly from the darkness of a screw's turn up to an iron ladder and the seat of a goateed attendant; after sharply scrutinizing you and suspiciously examining your carelessly crumpled ticket, holding it up to the light, testing it between his fingertips, and scanning it at an angle for the presence of a secret pass sign, he hands you a wooden token as big as the palm of your hand which another, even more goateed, attendant ensconced beyond the top of the iron ladder in a sort of cage then exchanges for an artfully folded little cotton bag, a metal tag with a key and, to show the way, a wave of the hand of such – albeit vague –

grandeur that, thrust into a twisted and tangled ghetto-like thicket of cage upon cage formed by lathes, lattices, staves, grilles, slats, slits, joists, joints, holes and air, numbered with unholy abandon and finding yourself in the one cage that is perspicuous from all sides and hence unfathomable, in this labyrinth of passages, nooks, crannies, angles, cubbyholes, corners, alcoves, cubicles sprouting sties and stalls, you don't at once capitulate but, still hoping to find your own you wander on through the stalls, sties, alcoves, corners, cubbyholes, angles, crannies, nooks and passages of this unfathomable – although perspicuous from all sides – labyrinthine cage of cabins sprouting cagelike over cages between cages, numbered with unholy abandon and formed by air, holes, joints, slits slats, grilles, bars, staves and lathes, a twisted and tangled ghetto-like thicket, until, since all your questions directed at the sheeted or loin-clothed fellow inmates evoke merely a voicing in German of your cabin number, you grasp that your confidence was but conceit and that you should count yourself lucky enough to find your way back to the attendant – when suddenly out of that very bend which you would have un-hesitatingly sworn you had already rounded five times, your cubicle looms up, smiling and large as life; and with a sigh of relief you enter, undress, stand naked, look around, peer out and descry beyond lathes and slats and slits between slats and slits and lathes nothing but sheeted and loinclothed figures and in your nakedness believe yourself to be once again at the end of your tether: once again to have to leave the cubicle you have finally found for the sake of a lousy loincloth and re-enter the twisted and tangled, lathed, staved, grilled, slatted, slitted, joisted, jointed labyrinth of cage-like cubbyhole grottoes cabins gratings canals gangways crannies grooves corners grilles cubicles of the perspicuous from all sides – no; and then, fully prepared to emerge naked you discover, as you decide to put away your valuables and unfold the little bag, that this little bag is not a little bag but an apron, a loincloth made of gray cotton to be tied around the hips with a piece of string; this you grasp, you do it and, like everyone else, with your nakedness covered you walk out with a sigh of relief and realize that you, for it is you, are lost: you will never find your cubicle again, the cubicle with your passport and all your money and all your papers, but by now it's too late, no bend appears, the stream takes hold of you and washes you into the unknown and, abandoning yourself to your fate and cursing the 'flu that has so thoroughly sapped your will, you drift along in the stream, protected in front, exposed behind, and now the flotsam is sorted: loincloths only, no sheets, the labyrinth narrows down to a passage, and the passage winds its way, ever more crooked and narrow into the maw of Hell: clouds of steam, aura of sweat, rising vapors, drifting mist, swaying lights, gliding figures, gasping and rumbling, pillars looking like wraiths, grottoes, caves, steps going down and up and pools with heads and fluttering hands, the floor is slippery, the steps are slick, the walls feel greasy, you slip and grab at wood and grasp a bolt and with a creak a door opens and you stop dead: There, in boiling dry air, assembled around their lord Álmos, sit the Hetumogens. ...

"Valóban nagy tudós vagy, idegen. ..."

It is indeed they, the Hetumogens, the heroes of the land seizure, the seven vassals of Álmos, brown-skinned Magyar warriors, most of them silver-haired, a fine sweep to their mustaches, in their eyes the gaze of the turul falcon; they recline on seats fit for heroes, wooden chairs with wide arm-rests to support in comfort arms wearied by sword and reins, while they hearken to the words of their lord, for he who is addressing them is Álmos, son of Eleud, son of Ugeg, son of Ed, son of Chaba, son of Ethele, son of Bendeguz, son of Turda, son of Scemen, son of Etei, son of Opus, son of Kichids, son of Berend, son of Zulta, son of Bulchu, son of Bolug, son of Zambur, son of Zamur, son of Leel, son of Levente, son of Kulche, son of Ompud, son of Miske, son of Mike, son of Beztur, son of Budli, son of Chanad, son of Buken, son of Bondofard, son of Farkas, son of Othmar, son of Kadar, son of Beler, son of Kear, son of Kewe, son of Keled, son of Dama, son of Bor, son of Hunor, son of Nimrod, son of Thana, son of Japhet, son of Noah, who floated across the Flood to Mount Ararat. ... They are the ancestors of Hungary, and Álmos speaks to them about his mother's dream of a torrent of water issuing from her that turned into a river in a far-off land, and Álmos speaks of the land with the greenest grass and the blackest soil and the mealiest grain and the sweetest water, and they nod their heads, the seven lords, the seasoned warriors: Árpád nods, father of Zoltán, father of Toxum, and Zobolch nods, father of Chak, and Gyula nods, father of Gyula, father of László, and Cund nods, father of Kusid and of Czupan, and Leel nods, who drove the Bohemians from Golgotha, praised be his name, and Werbulchu nods, and Urs also nods, and Werbulchu beckons to the stranger standing humble in the entrance to come forward and close the gate, and Gyula, father of Gyula, father of László, father of Sarolt of the starlike beauty, points to the seat at the end of the gathering –

        – but then the noblemen, shocked out of their musings, start up, up jumps Álmos the Old and Árpád the Bold and Zobolch the builder of castles and Gyula, father of Gyula, father of László and

father of Sarolt of the starlike beauty, and up jump Cund
and Leel and Werbulchu and Urs with the longest beard
under his chin, up they all jump and furrow their brows
and eight times two eyes flash steel and wrath at the
stranger, who has dared to remove the loincloth from his
nakedness to spread it over the moisture covering the seat
of the chair and who now, crimson with embarrassment,
turns and flees

Among pillars, in niches, under arcades: four pools, three
large, one smaller, one shell-shaped, one shaped like a
stadium, the water rising in temperature from the smallest
to the largest pool each time by four degrees, from twenty-
eight to forty degrees Centigrade, and on the water in the
circle of the talking heads, bibs floating like lotus blossoms

Thirteen Leopold Blooms: what a metamorphosis

In the sauna: the old men have left, and now above the
common people an athlete sits on the arm of a chair, wring-
ing himself out. Doggedly, as stubbornly solemn as an
athlete who has come in eleventh at the regional champion-
ship, he squeezes the water out of his tissues, pore by pore,
and every time he lifts his elbow he ripples the muscles of
his arm, and no one pays any attention, wise nation! For
fifteen minutes he works the section between collarbone
and the top of his left breast, I might have been curious
to see whether he kept up this pace, but the heat drives
me out

And in the heart of the turning screw, in the sacrificial pit
between two massive short stairways, waits the Minotaur
with a smile: a youth, handsome and black as only a
Pasiphaïde can be, he stands there bare to the waist in the

middle of the pit, and all must pass by him, the loincloths drop, the victims stand naked, and with a smile he rejects them and in his compassion hands each one a sheet to cover all his nakedness

and you enter a huge hall where on four pallets lie forty shrouded bodies, motionless and pale and hideously groaning, while up front lurk four trimmers, their scissors agape, and you too must pass them, you too

and past the pedicurists and again through another hall, this one impressive and empty, you return by way of the tiled passage as it unwinds from the night and, serene in your sheet, climb past the attendant and up the ladder to the next attendant, while two awkward intimidated newcomers present their tickets

and once again you risk losing your way in the labyrinth; when you ask the attendant in the cage how to reach your cubicle, he merely relieves you of the metal token and generously repeats his generous gesture toward the landscape of lathes and lattices, but then Gyula, father of Gyula, father of László, father of Sarolt of the starlike beauty, takes you by the arm and leads you, and suddenly your cubicle is there, and in it, wonder of wonders, jacket and trousers with money and passport and all your papers, and Gyula, father of Gyula, father of László, father of Sarolt of the starlike beauty, asks eagerly: "What's Kunert been writing recently

and through the resting area where perspiring old men sit in coats and hats (to whom after this odyssey and, although you lack coat and hat, you now also belong), and through the exit marked ENTRANCE to the outside, and then the courtyard slips from under me; I have to sit down, and now I'm really scared about making my way home, but then Ferenc appears, yes indeed: these baths are Hungary's academy. Ferenc has phoned for a taxi and now sits beside me on the bench in the fresh air and blows the smoke of his Terv under my nose; I cough and cough and wave away the cloud of smoke, and Ferenc says sympathetically: "Yes, 'flu is a horrible thing, you can't even stand smoke," and, lighting a fresh cigarette from the old one, he moves closer and asks whether it is true that György said Gábor had told him that I had said to Elga that I was writing a book about Budapest, and he emphasizes the last few words with such cutting skeptical irony that in spite of my fever and annoyance I laugh out loud: Don't worry, Ferenc, don't worry, I don't even feel competent to write so much as an essay about one of the bridges, I'm keeping up my diary, that's all, and if particles of Budapest are reflected in it, it's not Budapest

That evening at Elga's for *paprikáskrumpli* and *bableves* made of huge broad beans with tiny home-made dumplings, the latter a specialty of the youngest son, the mathematician (the oldest one is, like his father, a musician). The main course is a peasant dish: large chunks of potatoes, large chunks of sausage, large chunks of smoked meat, large chunks of paprika, all braised together, in lard of course, the spices are a secret of the hostess, and I eat and eat

Ferenc finds fault with my expression "peasant dish" as smacking of operetta; I should read Móricz, he insists, then I would find out what a Hungarian peasant eats

"Paprikáskrumpli," says Elga, "that's what Grass Günter had here, he ate two large platefuls, then he helped himself to a third, that's when we stopped eating and just watched Grass, but he also polished off the third plate, then he helped himself to a fourth, and at that point I thought, I can't let this go on, he'll burst, but then my curiosity won out and I let him go ahead, and so he got through the fourth plate too!"

"And then?" I asked eagerly, and Elga beamed as she said: "And then he had some salami and cheese

The youngest son, the mathematician, leaves us early: he is going off at the crack of dawn on a day excursion to Vienna. "Does he get a day off for that?" I ask, and Péter tells me the whole class is going, and noting my no doubt bewildered expression Elga says: "Look, it's in our interest to see that our young people get to know the world, they'll have to find their way around one day and not look like fools representing Hungary, so they can't start early enough to gather experience!" (The musician is studying in Leningrad

Look up at home who first said: "An Austrian has no business going abroad!"

Mándy's stories: Such stuff dreams are made of, dreams and days of Joseph Town, of District VIII, the most modest of modest quarters. I only know this southeast district beyond the Great Ring from Mándy's stories; the stranger is no more likely to go there than a stranger in Berlin to Acker Street, and it is exactly the kind of world to which I wanted to escape in my young days and that remained barred to me no matter how avidly I sought the key

At the time, when at school in Reichenberg, that sudden love: the girl going around with the collection plate after the tightrope act; I had a fever then too, I was ready to throw my whole month's allowance onto the plate, and then I felt ashamed, and felt ashamed at the very idea of giving money, and fled, and her curses followed me

World at the outermost edge of the bourgeoisie where the domains of Hoffmann and Gogol begin

I remember the children playing in the gutter of Hübner Lane when I first went to secondary school in Reichenberg; they were much younger than I and I stood there in my sailor suit envying them and wanting to join them in fishing scraps of paper out of the drain, while indoors at Makosch & Makoschek the sight of my father haggling over the price of a pair of knickerbockers had filled me with such rage and embarrassment that I ran out of the store

This world was for me the Other, and the Other had to be the genuine. ... The world I lived in was the world of lies. No greater lie than those Christmas Eves when the maid sat, awkward and blushing, at the family dinner table while her mistress served her, and her master, who had had to be brought home from the tavern, sang "Silent Night, Holy Night" and the candles glowed. ... The Christmas tree reached from the floor to the ceiling; we had fish soup, baked carp, red wine, torte, coffee and home-made chocolates, then the family would go to mass, and then the maid put on some more clothes, she had to do this when she went to bed because it snowed into her little back room

World of daydreams, of vows, of sacrifices, of illusions, where faith, hope and charity were worn so thin yet never became shabby

World of rebellions, of revolt, of insubordination: with what tremors of ecstasy I would watch the flames from the crematorium, which had been built near our village by a society for cremation and free thinking. In our Catholic area they were the breath of Lucifer, they roared against God and defied Hell

Or in Reichenberg the Shepherds' Inn down in the valley, that was the tavern with the worst reputation, we never dared go in, we never dared even go close, and often, at dusk, we would stand above by the football fields and look down and clutch one another and stand very still, and the Malay emerged from the torture chamber

In Mándy (what do I mean: "in Mándy"? All I know of him is this little volume of five stories) there is not a grain of sentimentality. These stories are crystals: hard, sharp-edged, clear, precise; unfathomable

Mándy: "One afternoon Uncle Barna threw his hospital gown around his shoulders. In the washed-out robe he looked like some seedy assassin now reduced to accepting piddling little contracts."
  Or: "The daughter was eating, she did not even look up from her plate. With her thick, blond hair, her tanned arms, she looked as though she were sitting on the edge of a swimming pool."

No, that conveys nothing. You can't quote anything from Mándy

World of the grotesque: poverty grotesque, hunger grotesque, plans grotesque, crimes grotesque, pain grotesque, desire grotesque, complaints grotesque, physiognomies grotesque, and the grotesque so horrifyingly real – was it this that attracted me

It was simply the Other. ... Of course the Other within my own world, otherwise it could not have been dreamed of. And not the working class: between it and me stood that vast gray dully roaring man-eating Moloch, a few hundred yards across from my father's house: the Haney factory

Strange, or perhaps not strange at all, that this other area was also always the area of freaks, of hunchbacks, midgets, the deformed, the blind, the deaf and dumb, the twisted, the crippled, the halt and the lame. The workers all looked normal, only paler, skinnier and grayer: the Other could not possibly be there

Is compassion merely reactionary? To this question there are some generalized affirmative answers, but any feeling, even hatred, can weaken or strengthen social energies, and any emotion, as long as it is honestly and strongly felt, can generate strong and honest literature, which in itself constitutes social action

And of course compassion is not pity, let alone self-pity. *That*, be sure, is repulsive

Tradition of Gogol, Dostoevski, Chekhov, Gorki, Jean Paul, Barlach, Laxness and Kazantzaki; one shouldn't be in such a hurry to turn up one's nose

The words "hackneyed," "worked to death," contain tragedies. ... The victims have already been removed, the scourges are still lying in the corner, their ends tattered and blood-clotted

"Worked to death" – in the "o" we see the last swelling of the exhausted biceps of the whipmaster

"To be between" – this is ambiguous: barrier or connection

$S = P$ – the equal-sign is between the two
$S \neq P$ – the irreconcilable sign is between the two

Jean Paul's *Attila Schmelzle*: we laugh at him for being a milksop, but what cries out from within him, so shrill and absurdly helpless, is that fear which later isn't funny at all, the fear known also to Woyzeck and his captain

and also the new characteristic of subservience: the tragi-grotesque subservient

Schmelzle attempts desperately to avoid the fate of a K. Three days and two nights of this attempt are recorded, and they are terribly funny; of the subsequent ones we know nothing

That fear of the Outer *and* of the Inner: to be sitting in the crowded church below the pulpit and suddenly feel the irrepressible urge to shout up to the preacher: "I'm here too, Reverend. ..."

Or to be passing a prison in a strange town and thinking that someone inside is rattling at the bars and shouting, as he points down at you: "Down there goes my accomplice. ..."

That other Attila, that so very different Attila, the author of the Song of Solidarity, knew this fear too: "I shan't escape my punishment!"

And with what howling of the heart was *Wutz* written

And the words of the dead Christ, clothed though they are in consolation, represent the most dismal funeral oration for the sound world that I know

"And when I looked up to the immeasurable world for the divine eye, the world stared back at me out of an empty, bottomless eye socket; and eternity lay upon the chaos and chewed it up and rechewed itself. ..."

Jean Paul and Ernst Barlach – that might be a topic

Or finish the *Comet*

More modestly: a little volume of dreams

Whether Mándy's Joseph Town is the heart of Budapest may be open to dispute, but the heart of Joseph Town is indisputably the Pantheon Cemetery, where Hungary's genius lies a hundredfold

The execution of the Hungarian hussar in Jean Paul's *Fälbel* and the execution of the partisans in Jünger. ... The reciting of these two passages could replace an entire course of lectures. ... Both passages contain the same mythologem, and how utterly different is the telling: here by the plebeian democrat, there by the aristocratic fascist! That *one* class can fly on such irreconcilable wings

My behavior at the taxi stand was shabby. ... But what else

should I have done? That's not really the question. What was shabby was my reaction of contempt while making no effort to understand the baggage helper, just that and just there. But isn't it the action that matters? Yes, the next one

(and again for the sake of the next action: "By all means take on the task of a partial function. ..." I can't get away from this phrase

The baggage helper was a citizen from the world I hankered after. ... I never attained it, and now I shall never (and do not want to) attain it. I have left the old world behind

Where am I

Only twice was I actually "within it," completely within it, in complete, blissful harmony, and in both cases I was on the periphery: behind barbed wire at the Antifa School [the antifascist training school for prisoners of war] and during my time at the Warnow shipyards

Twice: that's quite a lot. The general rule is: not even once

In the building across the lane, the shutters otherwise always half open and aslant are suddenly closed, a fantastic transformation

October 22

Slept late, feel a bit better

Away with you, night thoughts

Across the lane the shutters are again half raised, their lower edge slanting toward the windowsill like a fan

and the Devil is moving into Budapest: through Magyar Street a sulphur-yellow van drives slowly along with the pitch-black inscription
APOLLYON

What is the Tempter doing in Budapest, where does he come from, where does Marguerite live? His black cat has preceded him everywhere

Apollyon drives down to the Danube; to Margaret Island, where else? And now I remember that Gellért Hill used to be known as Witches' Hill

In the corridor the smirking chambermaid: is she already aware of the Tempter's arrival? Even the fat old woman in the ironing room trills away flirtatiously

Imagine the following sentence: "In the corridor the smirking room tender."
    M. would say: The language is having its revenge

The waiter has twirled the ends of his mustache; he walks busily up and down rubbing his hands, in his eyes a yellow light as he surveys the unsuspecting diners

Newspaper item: Scientist run over by streetcar

In the hotel lobby, sudden shouts and screams

The red telephone rings incessantly

Smoke pours out of the kitchen

The sky turns milky black, pregnant clouds gather, swarms of flies, midges, lice and cockroaches descend and dissolve over the roofs

Two plump red-haired girls hurry arm in arm down to the Danube

and a young man shouts excitedly: There, up there! brandishing a finger into the empty air, and everyone stares up into the sky, eyes flashing

and someone walks invisibly with iron tread, it is Ady's soul, whispering in fierce ecstasy: Strange things will come to pass, strange things will come to pass

In a small gathering of the Authors' Association, a discussion on morals in literature; the Hungarians took it for granted that the concept of the writer as the diagnostician of society was the only possible premise for discussion. I find this definition both too narrow and too broad: generalizations of individual aspects never correspond to the whole, although each single aspect is important and reveals something of the essence

The moral element in literature today seems to me to be everything that aims at democratizing society. In the widest sense of the word: enlightening. ... Of course it does not follow that the writer must be a moralist. I suppose I am one

Did Apollyon pass by? Did Marguerite fly along Nép-köztársaság Street? Suddenly a depraved mental image that is hard to dispel and from it the idea for a double story: "The Dirty Saint" and "In a Wholly Clean World

Not far from the Astoria, an Austrian bistro; with Zoltán for some liver-dumpling soup and boiled beef; as we pick up knife and fork, each reminds the other of the famous description of an Austrian Sunday dinner in Joseph Roth's *Radetzky March*

Zoltán soon gets up to leave, he is expecting Apollyon – it happens to be the name of a delivery service

In my room tried to translate József's *Rebellious Christ*; stared stupidly at the paper for two hours, doodling little men. That's inevitable, at last I've realized this; my brain switches from one job to another with almost creaking laboriousness

Madách's tragedy of mankind: God as King Lear, the Devil as Cordelia. ... The editor refers to Job; he wishes, and rightly so, to refute the cliché of the "Hungarian Faust," but he overlooks the fact that, in contrast to Ma-dách, in the Book of Job the angels do not praise God and the Devil is a genuine partner

Madách has been accused of historical pessimism. But we must never forget that Madách narrates the story of the world from the viewpoint of the Devil. And he sees the

Devil not as a revolutionary but as the opposite of an idealist and, since God is inevitably the stronger, we should be more inclined to give the Devil his due for optimism

October 23

My principle of treating myself, even when I am sick, as if I were well will no doubt be severely tested today

My brain has made the switch: almost unawares, the first verse of the József poem is there, but after that I am exhausted

Persistence does pay off: salt sticks for breakfast, and a double portion of coffee in the pot

An article on environmental protection and pollution: all those things we were so proud of even ten years ago: traffic, fumes, stink, noise, at one time every city's badges of distinction, are now being outlawed. But here too: the difference between "not yet" and "no longer." Imagine your Berlin, Unter den Linden at noon, and someone proudly proclaiming: Look, our latest achievement: so-o-o little traffic

Off to the covered market: twice before I have wanted to do a piece on it; if I don't this time, I'm sure I never will

First impression: cathedral of steel. Seven naves, pillars, columns, huge windows and tracery, galleries, and the crowds no more reverent than in any other cathedral. But that's as far as the image goes; the most important characteristic is lacking

Better: a railway station, on the tracks stand overflowing freight trains. ... Steel, glass, milling crowds, electric carts, people loaded down, green and red lights – this might very well be a cousin of Western Station

Strangely quiet, only a low hum, the murmur of those buying and selling; no noise; no arguing; no touts either, the merchandise must speak for itself. Even the *vigyázz* shouts of the electric-cart drivers are subdued, meant only for the immediate obstacle

Lengthwise symmetry: a broad central aisle flanked by stalls; on either side and parallel to the main aisle, a narrow second aisle and a somewhat wider one: and at right angles to these aisles, after every three stalls or so, transverse aisles, making nine altogether. All around the second floor an inside gallery with two transversals and protected by iron grilles over six feet high in some places. Above the main entrance a buffet. Walls of iron, tile and glass right up to the louvered wooden roof spanning the hall in a gentle curve of eight ocher-colored sections

Food only is sold, upstairs flowers as well (and flowers at each entrance and in every corner). Along the central aisle mostly meat, bread, cheese, pastries; at the far end and spreading out to the parallel lanes and rising in great waves up the walls: the sea of fruit

At the very end the mushroom stalls: shaggy manes, hawk fungus, green agarics, milk fungus, giant parasols, tricholomas, all halved and still trudging along the shelves in single file as once they did in the forests

Yellow barrels of pear juice – the pears; red tubs of apple meal – the apples; golden-brown goblets of onion tang – the onions; detonating caps of pungency – the paprikas

Mountains of brain-white walnut meats and moon-white hazelnut meats; in shallow bowls every type of lentil and bean; snow-white mounds of garlic, snow-gray ones of potatoes; root stems of horse radish and celeriac; thunder clouds of eggplants; fairy grottoes of pumpkins. ... Radishes the size of your fist, turnips the size of your head, carrots as thick as your arm, cauliflower as large as your belly; little coal-black radishes, little honey-yellow lemons, little grass-green cucumbers, blood-red tomatoes, sea-green cabbage, delicate green corncobs, mat-green spinach, emerald-green apples, reed-green paprikas, green-gray Alexander pears, amber-yellow grapes, olive-yellow grapes, olive-green grapes, opal-yellow grapes, rainbow of soup greens, iridescence of bunched herbs, palette of bowls filled with spotted, dotted, speckled, stippled, mottled, dappled, marbled broad beans of every conceivable color; the walls of the booths shiny red, shiny green, shiny black, lanterns of yellow apples, garlands of paprikas, and crowning all a strident, gaudy, man-size rooster

In glass tanks pretty, pouting fishes

Eggs in bushels, eggs in baskets, eggs on racks, eggs in bowls, eggs upon eggs upon eggs upon eggs, and not cracking under their own weight

Seen from above: a sea of every color, only blue is missing: the plum season is over, so are the blue and green grapes. In town you can still buy plums, but already they have a touch of frost and the market hall will not carry such items

No red cabbage, no savoy cabbage, no oranges, no bananas – in short: nothing exotic

And now is a very bad time anyway, Jutta tells me, for describing the covered market: There are no – and in summer

and early fall the market is bursting with them – straw-
berries, no raspberries, no currants, neither black, white,
yellow nor red, no blackberries, no blueberries, no goose-
berries, no rose hips, no asparagus, no lettuce, no peaches,
no apricots, no greengages, no yellow plums, no whiteheart
cherries, no sour cherries, no cornelian cherries, no Bing
cherries, no watermelons, no muskmelons, no woodruff, no
chanterelles, no boletus, no redcap mushrooms, no birch
mushrooms, no marron mushrooms, no goatsbeard, no
giant puffballs, there is simply nothing, nothing whatever,
why was I wasting my time

I stand by the balustrade on the upper floor and write and
write and write, and no one even bothers to look around
at me

In the first transversal: *Yellow Submarine*. ... This is where
the ducks reside, and everything here is yellow: yellow
meat, yellow fat, yellow beaks, yellow feet, yellow innards;
interspersed with pasta, also yellow: yellow noodles, yellow squares, yellow shells, yellow macaroni, at the rear
yellow brooms, yellow brushes, yellow baskets, and even
the flowers at the intersection of the two aisles

Imagine someone stationed there to sort people out as to
whether or not they fit into the yellow world and raising
them up or casting them down accordingly

"You have to let *me* in – look, I have a doctor's certificate
to prove I'm liable to jaundice

And how Envy would puff itself up and look down in
scorn on Hope or Faith

The second transversal: the scruffy corner. The stalls consisting of only one or two rough boards supporting a jar or two of sunflower seeds; a few blackish garlic bulbs, a few blemished apples; a terribly thin duckling straight out of Hans Andersen

Inconceivable that anything is sold here. But why do the country women come here? Is there a reason? Is it a status symbol

An old peasant woman nonchalantly adjusts her garter of wide, knotted elastic

Downstairs again: and on three almost vertically rising racks of Jonathans, Coxes and Gold or Permains is to be seen the abundance of the year from strawberry red to gooseberry purple

The customers carry shopping nets, and the varied hues are repeated kaleidoscopically. The purchases pile up higgledy-piggledy in the nets: potatoes, eggs, cauliflower, sausage, cakes, lemonade, and each tolerates the other and nothing gets broken

So many berets, in fact so many men shopping, how strange it seems

Fish: reddish gray, reddish silver, silver-gray, silver-black, black-gray, but merely the substratum beneath the luster made up of all this and with a blush, the color of blood, predominating

Outside am overcome. ... Hot sun, strong wind, one last effort, otherwise I shall have to see a doctor tomorrow.

I walk a little way along the Danube, take off my coat, jacket and shirt and lie down on the river bank

So: beside this city, by the water, on the rocks, a few children, who ignore me, are fishing close by: this would be a good place to draw a balance sheet. In a few weeks I shall be fifty. What do I have to show for it? How have I fulfilled my partial function

On Freedom Bridge, hobbling along on crutches, a beggar, his left leg amputated below the knee, his right leg in a steel brace. The man is short, hunchbacked, his face bloated, his upper lip eaten away, his gray bony skull, when he uncovers it, revealing a sizeable dent. On reaching the projecting bay around the outside of the pylon, downriver on the Buda side, the beggar stops, angrily surveys the windswept ground, with an oath uses a crutch to knock a bone onto the roadway and, his back to the railing, lowers himself to the ground with a groan. He has his place and makes use of his day

Observe the way he accepts the coins. ... No, don't look at him at all, don't give him anything either

Where to start with the balance sheet? From "my function," of course – but who has allotted it to me? Society, the critics and, later, literary history, or is it the sovereign choice of the author as individual? For each writer it can only mean: that particle of literature which he and he alone can write. In this sense he is indispensable (provided always that what he creates is literature), and it is this indispensability that society, too, should take as its premise

The waiter at lunch, and the way he accepts his tip: just as you are about to put the coins on the table he emerges from the kitchen and, ignoring you completely, heads for a table near the exit. You would not dare detain him were you not encouraged, by a barely perceptible nod, to assume that you and only you are at liberty to importune this busy man. You hand him the coins; casually, without looking down, he slips them into his pocket, while at the same time, without slowing his pace even a fraction, he proceeds imperturbably toward the end of the room; there, with gentle strokes, he gives the corner of a serviette the final touch and, as you leave, acknowledges you with a smile and a bow, the depth of which corresponds exactly to the size of your tip

Breaking out in a sweat; vertigo; relief

No heart to work; no heart to go out; no desire to read, no desire to eat, expecting no one, expected by no one: so what do you do? Compose a little concrete poetry

POINTSPOINTSPOINTSPOINTSPOINTSPOINTS
POINTSPOINTSPOINTSPOINTSPOINTSPOINTS
POINTSPOINTSPOINTSPOINTSPOINTSPOINTS
POINTSPOINTSPOINTSPOINTSPOINTSPOINTS
POINTSPOINTSPOINTSPOINTSPOINTSPOINTS
POINTSPOINTSPOINTSPOINTSPOINTSPOINTS
POINTSPOINTSPOINTSPOINTSPOINTSPOINTS
POINTSPOINTSPOINTSPOINTSPOINTSPOINTS
POINTSPOINTSPOINTSPOINTSPOINTSPOINTS
POINTSPOINTSPOINTSPOINTSPOINTSPOINTS
POINTSPOINTSPOINTSPOINTSPOINTSPOINTS

$P_{O_I}N^T$ $P_{O_I}N^T$ $P_{O_I}N^T$ $P_{O_I}N^T$ $P_{O_I}N^T$ $P_{O_I}N^T$

Points

$p_{\ o}^{\ i}\ _n{}_t$

POINT
POINT
POINT
POINT
POINT
POINT
POINT
POINT $P^{O}{}_{I}{}^{N}{}_{T}$
POINT   woof – POINTER
POINT   woof –   POINTER
POINT   POINTERPOINTERP$^{O^I}$
POINT
POINT   P O   IN

The point   The pointer

Variations II

```
    i          un        b
  o   n      l    t        l
 p     t    b      s        u
point      blunts            e
                            s
point      blunts    blues
point      blunts    blues
point      blunts    blues
point      blunts    blues
point      blunts    blues
point      blunts    blues
point      blunts    blues
point      blunts    blues
point      blunts    blues
point      blunts    blues
point      blunts    blues

point      blunts    blues
```

			BLUES OCKING
			BLUES OCKING
			BLUES OCKING
			BLUES OCKING
			BLUES OCKING
			BLUES OCKING
			BLUES OCKING
			BLUES OCKING
			BLUES OCKING
			BLUES OCKING
			BLUESTOCKING
			BLUESTOCKING
			BLUESTOCKING
			BLUESTOCKING
			bluestocking with run

Or this is fun too:

> At Esterhazy
> When Easter hazy
> Makes Esther hazy
> At Esterhazy

Dream:

Two men with white beards, in hobnailed boots, loden jackets and stocking caps, each with a load of freshly cut firewood on his back, enter the room and greet me. I know they are countrymen of mine, and I ask them to put down their wood and have a seat, but they shake their heads regretfully. We can't, says one of them, the taller one: or we might end up

losing it! Have you been lugging it around for long?
I ask, and the other man nods, and the first says
proudly: All the way from Bernau! I know that they
have been walking all the way and ask them what
was so special about the wood, it could be picked
up in any forest, and they both look at me in
amazement, and now the second man says: But it
was a gift

October 24

Recovery: full of shaky hope on tottery legs

Warm sun: with József's *Rebellious Christ* in my pocket, tapping rhythms and murmuring rhymes, out onto the Sunday streets in search of some quiet bench

Under the trees of Freedom Square: the paving stones covered with children's drawings: cars, buses, houses, kites, people playing ball, cats, cars and cars, cats and cats, and the ground plan of the world in the game of hopscotch

Fascinating thought: to return by increasingly difficult routes and increasingly difficult leaps to the starting point, and to chalk a mark at every station and wipe it out again

Behind closed shutters the American Embassy. ... The day before yesterday the Cardinal left by plane, and Zoltán says: "No one is happier about it than the Americans – to have a moralizer in your house for sixteen years without a break, who can stand that

Three more verses ready in rough draft, the most difficult bits while aimlessly wandering around, and rediscovering by chance, quite close by, the enchanting art nouveau building I have been looking for all these days

What a pity this building stands so tucked away, and so crowded by other buildings that no overall impression is possible – one should be able to stand back two blocks, and the lane offers hardly twelve feet. But out of the details grows the dream image of a whole city area of such architecture, and the art nouveau buildings of all cities assemble

Great butterflies of brick and concrete with scales of
      gold, green, red and blue
Pieces of mangled bodies, fallen from the sky after
      a battle of dragons
Petrified lotus blossoms on asphalt swamps
Rubble of the Jurassic
Rubble of the Limestone
Rubble of the Permian
Horoscopes for an air reconnaissance
Suras to delight Mohammed
Crowns for future archaeopteryxes
Designs for uniforms for a race of Anak's diplomats
Golden bosses and buttons
Golden anchors, dropped through the sea of the air
      to the bottom
Gilded slices of Swiss cheese
Leporello albums for onanists of Alpha Centauri
Guano of the angels
Rococo from retorts
Lowest rung of Jacob's ladder
Prisons of a 30th century
Mushroom saurians unfolding their umbrellas
Tigers enthroned on elephants
Citadels inviting an assault
Coat of arms of the emperors of Australia
Atolls of a minor flood
Ali Baba's treasure house
Beardsley's bookshelves
Coronation of the soap-bubble king
Children's toyshops
Sentry box of Gargantua's guards
Caparison corners among cambric pantalets
Antennas for receiving dreams

Thus stood the Red Sea on either side of the Israelites
Outer façades of the Mount of Venus
Here spake Scheherezade
Studios for my sculptor friends

Could one describe a street, a quarter, a city, a country by means of the thoughts, dreams, memories, feelings that come to one under their spell? Could someone else see those places from such jottings, would he recognize them, or could he visualize them? Certainly not a topographical image, but such notes do tell something about the spirit of the place

Emerging from a gray, peeling building, a little gray man ceremoniously carries an enormous cake across the empty street into another, equally gray building

Angels swinging on rusty-red, spiky rose garlands, and someone indoors is stumbling through Czerny studies with only one hand

Bearded fauns mocking bearded fauns

A very old woman in a mauve nightgown leans far out of her window

A façade with blue lilies, and across from it discovering that your wallet has been stolen

Little angels on swaying five-story-high columns, closing their eyes to avoid getting dizzy

Buildings that withdraw into themselves

Windows about to succumb to glaucoma

In the gable of a six-story façade, a recumbent white Apollo with a TV antenna sticking up between his legs. Out of the corner of his eye he looks down in disgust, as if he would like to spit on someone's head

There are certain localities whose image or, less specifically, description conveys a certain emotion to the public, for example: a sense of the sinister conveyed by the picture of a grim castle, or joy conveyed by a sun-filled forest glade. Nothing sinister need occur in the castle, yet sinister it seems. But are there emotions which a locality (or, to be more exact, a spot in Nature) is incapable of evoking? Does there exist a landscape, for instance, that evokes erotic feelings

Of course a natural object can appear obscene if it reminds one, say, of a sexual organ: certain fungi, for instance, or snails, or the tree in Mephistopheles' dream. But an obscene landscape

Is there such a thing as an exciting landscape? If the criterion for excitement is the prompting of the question, How does it go on? then exciting landscapes do exist – in the mountains, for example, in a grotto, at the bend of a river

Most certainly there are obscene landscapes in dreams

Jean Paul is the supreme teller of dreams, although his narrative technique must surely be the most unsuitable for this genre

The art nouveau buildings all have raised eyebrows and a superciliously wrinkled nose

Engels Square: two cars stop in the intersection, open their doors right and left and start a conversation, and the traffic cop strolls over to them and joins in

Comparison of an adjective not subject to comparison: "In Hungary Jean Paul is even more unknown than in German-speaking areas, where of all unknown geniuses he is the most unknown

In a little park: stone tables and stone benches for card players, and again: concentration; absorption; silence; almost no teenagers; no women. Piles of dried acacia pods; piles of swept-up leaves; leaves dropping soundlessly; cards dropping soundlessly

Movie: *The Anthill*, based on the novel of the same name by Kaffka Margit; a swarm of little nuns with a lot of naked bosom. The audience mainly women; next to me in thick plush a plump woman in her mid-sixties; grim struggle for the inch-wide armrest between our seats; my victory in the seventieth minute when, overcome by emotion, she reached for her handkerchief

Mándy has a whole volume of stories all set in old movie houses. How do I go about getting someone to translate them

The movie story told to me by Seryosha and how he wouldn't give up until he had found this movie house again, a dilapidated joint in Köpenick

The clown outside the burning building – unforgettable

And the flickering images of the battle cruiser on the curved wall of the Finnish tent in the POW camp in the Caucasian forest

And the hand with the finger reaching out toward me and pointing at me like the barrel of a revolver, in the center of my forehead mine alone among the hundreds and the thundering voice shouting in my ear Did you ever do that

And a willow tree, a willow of shadows, and mute, shadowy water, and I suddenly knew who Odysseus was

One of the movie house stories that I have wanted to write for years: it must have been 1943, in the summer, in Vienna, in my Rilke period, when the newsreel showed scenes from a concentration camp, and you saw three inmates wearing the Star of David and, obviously forming part of a chain, slowly passing rocks one to the other. ... The commentator remarked that the Jews were working for the first time in their lives, which was quite evident from the lightning speed of their movements, and the audience roared with laughter while I froze in horror, for we were looking at dying men reaching out with failing strength, receiving rocks from dying men and passing on rocks to dying men

It was Austrian laughter; laughter of my native land. ... To suffer because of Germany is bitterness; to suffer because of Austria is despair

Suddenly aware that one has recovered – how? By what one takes for granted: you can walk again for hours, coffee tastes as it used to, your thoughts play Ping-Pong again, in short, you're back to normal. But what is normal, what do we measure that against? Only against being ill, and that in turn we measure against being well. The normal is unimaginable without the abnormal, and vice versa

For one moment a cloud shaped like a bat

The abnormal – what is it? Two things: On the one hand, negation of the normal – you can't walk a hundred yards without breaking out into a sweat; coffee tastes all wrong, and so on. But there are other, independent, indicators that cannot be formulated as negatives, for example that stale taste in one's mouth, or the leaden feeling in one's limbs, or the buzzing in one's ears – that's not simply the negation of a healthy state, that's something new which, had you not experienced it when you were ill, you would never be able to imagine when you were well. Can one then say that illness widens your horizon? If you are experiencing it for the first time, certainly. As an example: people who are simply incapable of imagining a headache could never subscribe to Marx's favorite maxim: Nothing human is beyond my ken

But that would mean not merely that illness is the negation of health, but that it is more. Vice versa: is being normal, being well, also more than being ill, or is it merely the negation of all forms of being ill

But surely the fact that I can see is infinitely more than that I am not blind, or am I wrong

And surely the fact that I am blind is also infinitely more than that I can see, or does one "infinitely more" cancel out the other

Are there languages capable of expressing this difference: an ability (trait, condition) as an unproblematic datum, and then its self-renewal as a negation of its negation; thus: to see – and a seeing that includes the experience of being blind? Might German express it through intonation? Might Hungarian do it with its distinction between objective-subjective conjugation

The arch-conservative content of the phrase: "I'm my old self again!" And am I right in my feeling that the expression "Nothing's changed" was formerly used value-free whereas today it tends to be pejorative

The range of what is healthy (normal) has a definite, although not always sharply defined, lower limit beyond which the range of being ill begins – does it also have an upper limit? At a certain degree of reduced sharpness of vision I go to the ophthalmologist; but could I say: "Doctor, my vision is pathologically acute

However: "My hearing is pathologically acute" is a condition that some doctors might accept, and a hypertrophic sense of smell is without doubt a terrible disease

(And do proboscis animals also have a hypertrophic sense of smell, or is it that they cannot smell "acutely enough

A too acute vision plays a role in utopias, as, for instance, in the kingdom of the giants Gulliver sees the skin and breasts of his female guards

And Mistress Trude threw her child into the fire because its vision was too acute, because it saw the Devil in her swain

The inhuman begins above as well as below the human. So superman would be inhuman, as is the desire for him

Superlatives set full stops: so far and no farther! Anything going beyond must be a new quality and start again with the positive! A giant is bigger than a man, but the biggest man is not yet a giant, and giants are not the biggest men, they are gigantic

Each use of the superlative is a bit of pessimism: this is the summit, there's nothing beyond

The story goes that Tamerlane, in response to the boast of one of his relatives that in battle he could remain in the saddle eight days and nights without eating, drinking or sleeping, exclaimed: "In that case you must never be in command: how could you ever understand my warriors who must eat and sleep when their day's work is done!"

I always remember this anecdote when people like N. claim to be all-knowing and infallible supermen who know everything there is to know about all the philosophy, literature and art of all times and nations, to whom everything is clear, who are never faced with a problem, never have a question (unless it be inquisitorial) and so on and so forth. Supposing this were true: how could they ever be the very thing they claim to be – our mentors? How could they understand us normal human beings, us who struggle with problems, who know so little, who are sometimes confused, for whom sometimes the clearest things become clouded and who sometimes in that cloudiness see a bit clearer? And if they can't understand us, how are they supposed to lead

There is only one state of being well, but there are many

varieties of being ill. Can I say being well is the opposite of all forms of illness

Can I say that being well (normal) is that of which there is only one state? For that is the concept of the norm

Why are you put off by the above phrase when, as is legitimate, you reverse it: That of which there is only one state is the normal

Can I apply the concepts "healthy (normal)"/"sick" to society? Common usage does so, political powers of all persuasions also do so, but this implies a state of society (whether as ideal, in a utopia or actually present in reality) as being the only one appropriate to Man. This confuses you; you point to society as a historical concept and consequently to the necessity of seeing the term "health" as a social concept against a historical background. Yet the health, the normalcy, of an individual is also seen against a historical background: for an infant it is normal to lack sexual potency whereas for a twenty-year-old this would be abnormal and pathological. Can humanity as a whole also be regarded in that way, i.e., as a species developing from infancy to old age? Marx did so; he speaks of antiquity as being the childhood of mankind (which I find hard to emulate). But leaving this aside: we do say about a historic, concrete society, the bourgeois one of the present day, that it is sick, and you find this apposite. So what are the criteria for the socially healthy? For an answer we have plenty of generalizations, such as: a guarantee of the development of all human faculties; an opportunity for each individual to find himself, thus allowing him to live in a truly human manner, etc., etc. But what are the concrete criteria for all this

The dictionary of that clever Daniel Sanders defines "ill" as "the opposite of healthy" and "healthy" as "the opposite of ill"; look it up in *all* dictionaries

How do these dual concepts support themselves and one another? Are they the two poles of something which has a middle (which would then be "the normal"), or do they support each other in reciprocal attraction like two bodies in the universe; or are they crest and hollow of a wave that can cancel each other out

My vain attempts (but were they attempts, wasn't it primarily a wish, a desire, a goal) to describe what we call change! Change has been the experience of my life, my theme for twenty years, but it is in fact still no more than an intention, the most I have so far contributed toward it being the groundwork! I have described what preceded it, a little of what followed it, but I have not yet coped in literary terms with the crucial process, that of the change itself. I cannot find my way out of this thicket: in order to describe with credibility my first overpowering encounter with Marxism (with Marxism as a theory, as a spiritual experience, met with on my first reading of Lenin's writings on Lev Tolstoy and Lukács' sketches on the history of German literature when "the scales fell from my eyes"), I should first have described the state of mind of the young Fascist I really was. This in turn I could only depict against the contrasting background of the changed conception of the world, against the new, which, of course, I cannot very well depict convincingly as new without the old. Should one, could one, describe both against the background of a third (in the sense of the "middle" I just mentioned, or is there, to use Maiakovski's words, "no longer a middle in the world")?

And what do I mean by: "the Fascist I really was"? Until when was I that and up to what point? And in what relationship "until when and up to what point"? When I read Lenin I was reading him as a Fascist (although one who, granted, had passed through key experiences of Soviet reality, i.e., of Marxism in practice) – hence I was reading him "fascistically," and can such a thing exist: reading fascistically? I was, and I shall never forget it, touched as by a magic wand – what essential part of me was it that was so impressed? Was this being impressed part of being Fascist? Was it a sign of the fatal vulnerability of a contemptible world-view? Was it the first indication of the Other? Was it the posing of a contradiction? Or are we to assume the existence of traits common to all mankind, i.e., the "normal," and might that have been an earlier level which was covered over by Fascism and laid bare again by Socialism

Why didn't I join in the laughter at that movie

Metamorphosis – Queen of the Mythologems

(But don't take credit for that: after all, that behavior might just as easily be construed as failure, as unreliability

Begin at the beginning: a human being is born into this world. The yelling creature hanging there by the umbilical cord is without question totally uncommitted in the social sense: neither emperor, king, nobleman, townsman, peasant, beggar, nor capitalist, socialist, exploiter, exploited, revolutionary, reformer – merely a human being. Can one say: "This is the normal human being?" But this "normal human being" is still a long way from being just that; biologically speaking he does belong to the human species, whereas in social terms he has first to become a human being; a human being in the germ-state of humanity

My almost manic attempts to delve to the point where the social determining of the human being begins or, more concretely with regard to my own life, to the point of which I could say: From then on I was a Fascist. The answer seemed simple: Since the day I ran away from the monastery school, certainly no later than the summer of 1936. But the roots go much deeper, lost in voids of memory. ... On the other hand, certain typical characteristics of Fascist behavior and thinking developed very late in me, some of them – militant intolerance, for example – never fully

How could such typical characteristics be defined? In view of the inflationary use of the word "fascist" a precise definition seems necessary. Dimitroff's classic definition identifies the political aspect, but its manifestations differ greatly. Ideologically speaking the following seem to me to be common to every variety of the most recent past and present: elitist contempt for the masses combined with a desire to be absorbed in anonymity ("magic of four abreast"); militant nationalism combined with a striving to establish internationality; inflexible black-and-white thinking; glorification of what is brutal, cruel, bloody, primeval, combined with fascination for technology; desire to militarize all social – even personal and private – life combined with an affirmation of the anarchistic struggle of all against all; denunciation of reason, conscience and consciousness; leadership principle; demagoguery; fanaticism; extreme anti-Communism – and all of this together, not isolated

But surely the root is already the plant, and you eventually arrive at the infant, like Saint Augustine on his search for the origin of evil. For what you have failed to take into account is that, from its first cry and its first breath, this little bundle at the end of the umbilical cord is the son of one particular mother, the offspring of one particular family, the patient of one particular hospital, the citizen of one particular state, the member of one particular class and one particular nation; he will grow up in one particular nation; he will grow up in one particular sphere of ideology and culture; as he learns to speak he will absorb one particular world-image and is thus preconditioned – more strictly so, in fact, than he will ever be again (which does not mean he will be incapable of change

Can one penetrate prelinguistic regions by means of thought? That is too imprecise, what I mean is: can one express in language that which cannot articulate itself (even in an internal monologue)? Can one express what is going on in an infant when it smiles

It feels pleasure; yes, but how does it feel pleasure, how does it feel shock, or fear (does it feel fear at that age?), and so on. But then I have the greatest difficulty in describing my own fears – which I believe I know thoroughly – in such a way as to communicate them

Concretely: a four-month-old infant sees its mother approaching at bottle-time and stops crying and prepares itself in its own way for receiving the meal. That is undoubtedly more than a reflex, that is already a social response even if only a germ of one – can this "more" be articulated

Can we say what we cannot think? What, for instance, do we think when we say "ouch"? Are we thinking something, or are we saying something without thinking, something that we might also think, or are we saying something that cannot be grasped in thoughts? Of course I can think "ouch" in the sense that I utter this sound with my inner voice, but in that case I am not thinking "ouch", I am accomplishing inaudibly my intention to reproduce inaudibly the sound-complex "ouch

Do we *think* the difference between "ow," "ouch!", "oy!", "oooh!", etc., before deciding on one of these utterances? Can we *think* the difference (not: think *of* a difference)? And do we think "pff!" or "tsktsktsk" or "eeeeeee

My mother, when she sometimes tries desperately to voice a chain of thought she feels to be important: that gasping with wide open toothless mouth and the groping of the spread trembling hand, of the now barely visible lips, and then the collapse, the rasping, self-accusatory whisper: "If I could only say it, if I could only say it, it would be a revelation for you

A famous principle of modern logic, Goedel's principle, states more or less the following (my terminology will be hairraisingly inaccurate, but then I am not a mathematician and do not ask as a mathematician nor do I expect any answer from that quarter): imagine a certain system of clearly defined concepts, let us say: algebra. With these concepts, all of which are derived from the axioms of your system, you can form statements, and these statements must be either true or false, and it is this truth or falsehood that you must be able to prove. The statement, for example: "The sum of two even numbers is in turn an even number" is true. On the other hand, the statement: "Any number divisible by 3 must also be divisible by 6" is false, and the truth there and the falsehood here can be validly proved. And now, according to Goedel, there are statements, and there must be such statements, which are formed from the concepts of a system but cannot be determined within that system. According to our limited experience, our testings, our empiricism, they may appear to be true, but this truth has not been proved, it is still possible for a case to occur that would render them false, even if it occurred in the myriad-digital sphere (for instance, Goldbach's supposition that every even number that is greater than four is the sum of two odd primary numbers). In order to determine such statements, it is necessary, Goedel continues, to go beyond the system in which they have been propounded and construct a next-higher system. There such statements can then be determined; however, new statements emerge that cannot be determined, that in turn require a higher system for their determination and so on *ad infinitum*

To my mind, this statement – *mutatis mutandis* – seems of eminent significance for all spheres of human activity, not only for science. In order, for instance, to throw light on essential aesthetic phenomena I must go beyond the sphere of the aesthetic. But what system could go beyond Man

Consulted the dictionary – the word is "truism." This word annoys me; it should be "wise-ism." There are no important and unimportant truths

That rain falls down from above was a truism until Brecht made something of it

Paprika sausage with rolls –where in the world does this humble bistro get fresh rolls on a Sunday evening (no, not warmed up in the oven: fresh

And now remember that stale taste which as late as yesterday spoiled every meal for you – it is gone, and no effort of memory will bring it back. Now try to pinpoint it not as "stale" but concretely: "tasting of" – well, of what? It eludes you

Why can we not describe that stale taste more accurately? The "can" in this case is ambiguous – what can we not? Can we no longer recall it concretely, or can we not compare it because we are not skilled in metaphors in this field or because taste is too undifferentiated or because tastes as such cannot be compared or because in this particular case there is no alternative with which to compare it? Or for several of these reasons, or for all of them together

Can one say: adjectives are logograms of memories

Come to think of it, our imagination is very limited. What I have not experienced I can only know in the sense that I have stored secondhand information (hearsay) on that subject in my brain, information which could just as well be kept in storage for me by the encyclopedia. In another sense I do not know it: "I have no experience in this (of this; about this; in this field; with this; in this regard

But then I can also say: I know everything my encyclopedia knows! But without experience I know all this only to the extent that an encyclopedia knows it: it cannot act on the basis of what it knows

But when a technician employs a translation machine, can we say of him that he masters the language? Assuming that his computer is handy enough for him always to carry it around, we would have to answer Yes; indeed, someone who has never learned Hungarian might understand and speak Hungarian much better with his computer than someone who has struggled for ten years to learn the language. Why do we resist acknowledging this? Is it a dread of our personality being extinguished

But:

> "If I can buy six stallions fine
> Is not their strength then truly mine?
> I run and run, a man of pride,
> With four and twenty legs in stride."

That superman of Tamerlane's had never experienced the normal, and this was enough to make him useless as a comrade. As a lone scout he may have been without rival

That deeply humanistic meaning of the fairy tale about the boy who went forth to learn how to shudder: "Ah father," he replied, "I am most willing to learn something; indeed, if 'twere possible I would fain learn how to shudder: as yet I know nothing of that!"

In not knowing how to shudder, he felt he was lacking in a human dimension

Where does my experience show? In my actions. My language can simulate experiences, my actions cannot

And yet I can inject experiences, that's something this century has taught us! Offer worms their food variously illuminated and connect the blue light with electric shocks:

after a time the worms will avoid the blue food, and you can pass on their experience if you extract their nerve mass and inject it into normally fed worms. They will then act on this experience. But they will also avoid blue food when it is free of electric shocks – can such behavior be called "experience

Can it be said of this extracted substance: this stuff, this salt with such and such a chemical formula, of such and such specific gravity, such and such coefficient of water solubility, such and such a form of crystallization: that is an experience? Imagine a medicine chest of experiences for human beings; imagine it concretely: for young girls, for poets, for art politicians, for editors

Now raise worms that receive no electric shocks *only* with blue food, and inject a worm simultaneously with blue and anti-blue – what happens then? Do the experiences cancel each other out, or does the worm starve to death, or does something quite different happen

If one were to crystallize blue and anti-blue and dissolve them in a liquid in which they would dissolve – what would one call the substance contained in this liquid? One might label it: Any worm drinking this will turn into Buridan's ass

And now connect *all* the food with electric shocks – what happens then? Either the shocks kill the worm, in which case there is no experience to be bequeathed. Or the worm will acquire the experience that it is possible to eat even with electric shocks

The defiant attitude

Could there be experiences that, for whatever reason, cannot be injected? I don't really think so

Could we not regard such injections as prohibitions (or commands) together with their observance? Can we say of a salt, it is ethics

Across the lane the shutters are raised for a moment; the room is brightly lit, a luxurious room, rugs on the floor, rugs on the walls, easy chairs, chess table, TV set, bar, and the person raising the shutters and immediately closing them again is none other than Líliom

Irresistible desire to go out again: recovered

October 25

Dream:
**I am lying in hospital, about to have an injection.
The nurse sticks the needle into my upper arm, gives
me the injection, but then, while the needle is still
in my arm, she pumps the plunger up and down
several times, thus injecting air into the blood,
making it foam. I say in horror: For God's sake, what
are you doing, I'll get an air embolism! She says:
It's just to make it mix better, I've very rarely had
cases of air embolism, and if so you would be feeling
it within a minute! She goes on pumping, and I say
quite seriously: I have complete confidence in you**

In contrast to the German *wieviel*, in Hungarian there are
different expressions, one for "how many" and one for
"how much": *hány* asks what number; *mennyi* asks what
quantity. *Mennyi kenyér* – how much bread? *Hány kenyér* – how many loaves? Such possibilities of differentiation are the salt of the language; if they were lost, the language would be insipid. Just as we save endangered
species of animals and plants from extinction, so we should
protect endangered words and turns of phrase, e.g., the
positive with "as." "Like" compares the quantity, "as" the
quality; the difference between "I am as small as you" and
"I am small like you" is the difference between having the
same height and having the same authority

It would be valuable to establish the speed of linguistic
processes – the time elapsed between the first appearance
of a new form and its general acceptance (e.g., that ghastly
but irreversible "hopefully

And do those linguistic processes which you welcome (are there any? there must be) develop at the same speed as or at different speeds from those which, if you were Don Quixote, you would fight

As with numbers, in Hungarian "how many" takes the singular, and that reminds me of one of Wittgenstein's word-games, which he formulates as follows: "I send some-one shopping. I give him a slip on which are written the symbols: 'Five red apples.' He takes the slip to the shop-keeper; the latter opens the bin marked with the symbol 'Apples'; then he looks up the word 'red' in a table and finds a color chip opposite it; now he recites the series of numbers – I assume he knows them by heart – up to the word 'five,' and at each number he takes an apple from the bin that has the same color as the color chip."

So much for Wittgenstein; and here the plural would be unnecessary; the symbols on the slip would suffice in this form: "Five red apple" – and this is exactly the way the Hungarian says it: *"Öt piros alma"*! Of course, it would be entirely adequate to say: Apple red five (this word-order is not Hungarian

Moving, into a room with bath, almost an apartment! On the same floor, two doors farther along, facing the same street, and a completely new world

Ferenc is waiting for me in the lobby; I know he has an urgent appointment at the Ministry and I hurriedly trans-fer my belongings, I get into a sweat, feel a draft, and seem to be back at square one

The marble Metro; the large-eyed hostesses at the ends of the escalators; the freckled girl selling hot corn-on-the-cob. ... She doesn't say a word, nor do you, you wordlessly pay the correct amount, or she wordlessly gives change for three forints. I am tempted to give her too little to see whether she is really a mute, but I haven't the courage. I'm not made to be a reporter; why

Out into the sunshine into Líliom's city park; many baby buggies; many fat women; many old gentlemen; the air full of drifting autumn leaves. Three verses by József, then an art nouveau building, and what a beautiful one: the Castle of the Blue Flower

The little wall turrets with their blue fezes look as if they were humming Mozart

A cloud shaped like a lonely spinning-top, with no little girl, no little whip, no humming, lost in the blue, a symbol of immense forlornness

The remaining leaves in the green and yellow crowns of the poplars wave to the cloud, but it doesn't see them

Art nouveau buildings: window crossbars like harps

Followed by a tiny dachshund, a young couple, swaying in the fresh air, emerges from a tavern in the Mándy district. He in his Sunday suit, with Sunday shirt, Sunday tie, Sunday cow's lick; she, a head taller, in a tight orange nylon sweater above a crumpled knee-length brown skirt. He could be twenty-eight and she perhaps younger, although around the eyes and chin she is already beginning to wilt. They are both laughing as they come out, the hearty laugh at some cheeky suggestive remark; with a snort of laughter, one leg a step higher than the other, she collapses with her back against the wall, laughing so hard that she cries; with a chuckle he shakes his head and waves his hand toward the tavern door in a cheery gesture of refusal, a gesture that then turns into a sign to the dog.

Behind the grimy tavern windows, noisy drinkers stand around in dense smoke.

The dachshund hops down the steps and waddles over to a lamppost. The young woman, gasping for air, follows him with her eyes and tries to place a cigarette between her lips; the young man, one hand in his belt, the other in his pocket, shakes his head again with another chuckle, then, closing the door to the tavern, he calls: "Tóni!" and turns his heavy feet toward home.

The young woman is wasting matches.... Tóni lowers his leg, sniffs, scuffs the sidewalk, sniffs again, and prepares to go home, when a nondescript little old man, maybe sixty, maybe fifty, maybe seventy years old and wearing a packer's blue smock, emerges from a doorway; as he catches sight of Tóni, his gray papery face lights up, he gently snaps his fingers, and Tóni looks up.

"Tóni!" the woman calls, her cigarette finally alight in her mouth, "Tóni, *gyere!*"

Tóni pricks his ears to the right toward the snapping sound and to the left toward the call.

"*Tónikám,*" says the little man fondly. "Tóni mine, *Tónikám!*" He says it caressingly, like a tender declaration of love; he says it softly, but the place is so quiet that his whisper resounds. With an effort the young man turns around, and at the sight of Tóni wagging his tail at the little man he calls again with affable insistence. Tóni wags his tail. "*Mozgás, öreg fiú!* Come on, old boy!" – "*Tónikám!*"

Tóni scratches the ground as if wanting to bury himself to avoid making a decision, and the man and the little man look at him genially, full of shy affection, and they are about to exchange glances, and friendly ones, when the young woman has to laugh, and the look on the man's face darkens. "Tóni!" he calls roughly, "Tóni!" The dachshund twitches, stops scratching, and is about to waddle back when the little man takes a cube of sugar out of his pocket and, holding it out, steps forward, and Tóni follows him. The woman has pushed herself away from the wall. She is no longer laughing. "Tóni!" the man shouts, "Tóni, *gyere*!"

The little man stops, and Tóni stops. The woman, her cigarette in the corner of her mouth, leans with both hands on the knee of her bent right leg, looking as if she were still laughing inside herself. The man looks at her and sucks in air with a whistle. "*Kutyulikám*; doggy mine; *Kutyulikám, Tónikám*!" whispers the little man, then he puts the sugar back in his pocket, turns around, and walks slowly toward the doorway and Tóni follows him wagging his tail.

The woman, who up to now has been switching her gaze between the dachshund and the little man, throws a challenging glance at the man who, an instant ago, still swaying backwards, suddenly stands ramrod straight and motionless. The woman's eyes are glassy, her lips wet and bloated, her gaze lecherous. I am afraid that the man, standing like that, will topple forward, but he stands, stands motionless, stands for an eternity; then he utters, not very loud but quite clearly and soberly, a few words that I don't understand, and the woman's mouth slowly opens, her face becomes pasty, her lips twitch, he must have insulted her, and at that moment the little man turns around too. The dog whimpers in his desire for sugar and scratches greedily at the little man's legs, and that pathetic figure turns, pulling himself up to his full height, and raises a face full of righteous indignation toward the man. The latter rips open his collar, and now the pathetic one has also uttered a word, and the man, baying, dives forward in a rage. But by then the little man has disappeared into the doorway; a key is heard; Tóni wags his tail and scratches the ground at the man's feet, and the man gapes as if stunned toward the doorway, mutters something, straightens his tie and, paying no attention to the dog, walks to the tavern, passing the woman, who turns gray in the face, grabs her arm in passing and, without a word, drags her after him into the tavern, whence thick smoke comes belching out onto the street

In this story everything is conceivable, it is open on all sides, any ending is possible, from farce to murder

To be open in all directions: crucial junctions in life, points of possible change but also of possible non-change, and the sum of the portions traveled between such open points is the biography. The space in between need not be filled; it can be left open like the walls of a Gothic building; but a biography that did not contain all those open places, even if only one were lacking, would be seriously falsified

These open places could also occur in a straight line: then, as is commonly said, that particular life has been straightforward, but this straightforwardness was not inherent. Straightforward – meaning that the potential for change in direction was not tapped. Nevertheless, these stations of potential must not be left out. A biographical line is not a geometrical line: even as a straight line it is not determined merely by two points

Whether a person has moved from A to B, then from B to C and from C finally to D, eventually therefore from A to D, is not the same as if a person has arrived from A via F and E at D, although in both lines the starting and end points are identical. The intervening points must not be left out. The next step on the part of the first person might lead from D to E; the next step of the second person from D to C, and E and C might be in opposite directions. If only starting and end point had been visible, the divergent development would be incomprehensible. The entire line, the sum of all "open points," is the essence

The fact that a person will move from A via B to C and on to D is not inherent in A. From there the next step can go in any direction and, if it goes to B, all doors are once again open. There is no necessity to proceed from a certain childhood experience to a certain adult position; one *may* eventually arrive there, but there is no rule about it. This is a serious problem for the "I"-narrator who recounts childhood experiences from a point in adulthood, for this later stance must remain quite indefinite. If it is precisely fixed, and especially if it is an extreme stance, an impression of inevitability is aroused, and that is exactly what I want to avoid. I was very much tempted to tell some of my stories – the "Red Indians' Song," for example – from the stance of a member of the SS, but that would have reduced Fascism to the psychological level, and nothing would have been farther from my intention

If one says "A" one need not follow with "B," and if one does say "B" one need not follow with "C," and if one does say "C" one need not follow with "D," and so on up to F for Fascism. "A" can be the starting point for a great many things, but if the development started from A and ended, via whatever detour, at F, then A was the starting point for F

You might compare these open points with a turntable at a railway station: for the locomotive standing on it, all tracks are open. So far it has traveled on the track between A and B, and now it switches to the track C – D. Could this be called a change? In that case the locomotive would have to change, not only its direction! But the locomotive traveling from C to D is by that very fact different from the one traveling from A to B

Does anything change in the nature of a person if he changes direction in his life? This is the first time I have come upon this question; up to now I had taken it for granted and hence failed to notice the question which, I now find, permits a negative answer as well. No, it can by no means be taken for granted

And vice versa: can a person follow the direction of his life in an unbroken line and yet change? I could well imagine some such cases

Starting with a simple example: the secret services use the term "to turn around." A person is "turned around" – that would correspond to the image of the locomotive on the turntable. Someone has worked for A against B: now, "turned around," he works for B against A. Can this be called a change? I am tempted to say "no," yet I hesitate, although not as much as I would before a "yes

What do we mean anyway by: a person changes, is transformed, transforms himself? In what respect does he change (become transformed, transform himself), and in what terms: biologically, in health, in character, in spirit, ethically, religiously, ideologically, morally, politically, in party politics, socially, professionally, as a citizen, nationally, denominationally, in space, in time, as a phenotype, as a genotype, etc., etc. And what changes, what remains unchanged; and how does it change; are there types of change, relationship, similarity

If we say that X has changed, aren't we already saying that he has remained the same, otherwise we wouldn't have designated him by his name, as X

Change – process or result? These are two totally different situations! "S is becoming P" and "S has become P" is not the same! But "S is becoming P" must surely equal "S" for it is part of S that is becoming P. And "S has become P" must surely equal "P" for S has already been absorbed by P

What entitles us to say: "S is becoming P"? How do we know? If S has already become P, then it is not becoming P, then it is P; and if S is not yet P, then it is on the way to becoming it, but a lot can happen along this way

If we say: "Two and three equals five," would that mean a change of the two and of the three? Without a doubt, and a change of the five as well if we reverse the equation: "Five equals two and three

I still enjoy seeing numerals the way I saw them as a child: the 2 as a curtseying child, the 3 as a gentleman in a top hat, the 5 as a factory owner, the 1 could be anything, the 7 was a prisoner, I never liked the 4, it was a schoolteacher, snooping, brutal, given to violent rages and deceit.

And every equation was an adventure; "two and three equals five"—that was a fairy tale and a mystery, and only much later did I realize that beyond this it also meant something else, also the connection of sentences in books, indeed the connection of words in a sentence

The greatest mysteries, however, were the chemical formulas, some of their witchcraft exists for me to this day. ... I used to collect formulas the way some people collect beetles or stamps (we also collected and swapped car license numbers, we distinguished between nice ones and stupid ones, and we would never have dreamed of writing down a number we had not seen with our own eyes or swapped according to the rules), so I collected formulas like beetles, and I would sit far into the night over a fat alphabetical pharmaceutical book of my father's in my attic room, dreaming about the fate of a benzol ring

"Two and three equals five," that *is* a mystery. "Two and three" must be something other than "five," otherwise one could simply write "Five is five." But if it is something other, how can one write an equals sign? Patient Mr. D. explained it to me eight times, and each time I do understand it; puberty logistics, he says, and he's right, yet the ninth time once again I don't understand it

Do clouds really change? Does Proteus change, or is he that which changes, and in that case his change would be immutability

Puberty logistics, but amusing

"Do you see yonder cloud that's almost in shape of a camel?" – "By the mass, and 'tis like a camel ideed." –

"Methinks it is like a weasel." – "It is backed like a weasel." – "Or like a whale?" – "Very like a whale."

But Polonius is right, i.e., Hamlet is right, and Polonius
is right, since he agrees with him. That is exactly how
clouds change, exactly! But why do we take this scene as
evidence for Polonius's obsequious flattery of Hamlet?
"How now! A rat?"

But perhaps Shakespeare was using Hamlet's question
to test not Polonius but the judgment of the audience

Afternoon: a documentary film about Radnóti, disappoint-
ingly bad. I have not seen many Hungarian documentaries
so cannot generalize, but one cannot help wondering about
the reason for the discrepancy between them and the
magnificent feature films

I have the impression that these films treat the poet as
someone who must be flattered (reciting his poems, all
dressed up, in reverential tones). By doing so they inflict
the greatest possible harm on him

Lenin's saying about the proletariat, that it is not a young
lady at finishing school who has to be wooed

Across from us the Pantheon Cemetery; violent aversion
to visiting it

The story about Tóni, although a mythologem unfolded
within it, was a story for Mándy, not for me

On Rákóczi Street: a neon sign advertising lemonade

October 26

All morning at József's *Nagyon fáj*; seven verses fully completed in rough draft. In this ballad the most private emotions and, in them, the world: the spurned one summons all creatures that have been hurt to gather at the couch of the disdainful woman and to howl into her ears with all the voices of suffering: *nagyon fáj*, the pain is great; and there appear innocent people trampled by police boots, dogs that have been run over, castrated bulls, fishes on the hook, mothers giving birth, and the men. ...

> Double burden
> And double joy to be obliged to love.
> Who loves and cannot find a mate
> Is shelterless,
> As is exposed the creature of the wilds
> That has to stop to defecate.

At Gerbeaud's with Mándy. I tell him the story; he listens with rapt attention, gets more and more worked up, asks eagerly for the exact spot, what the couple looked like, the name of the dachshund, calls out: *"Jaj istenem!"* and, without waiting for his black coffee, jumps to his feet and races down into the subway

Mándy – a myth in a midnight-blue business suit

Why is Mándy so upset? Does he know the couple? Does he know all three? What is the role of the little man in the blue smock? How did the story end? I don't know

Whenever I see Mándy I remember some movie experience – this time the one about the speaker who at some ceremony or other seemed to think he was being filmed by TV and who immediately behaved the way he imagined a practiced public figure would behave when being filmed. He licked his lips to make them shine, smiled, sat up straight, slightly opened his mouth, raised his chin, squared his shoulders, looked strenuously past the camera, wrinkled his brow, leafed through his program, etc., no doubt dreaming of sitting in the evening with wife and child in front of the screen and calmly watching the amazement of his family. ... I saw him dream, for he stuck out his chest, his expression became majestic, and the whirring camera was filming the man behind us, and the TV that evening didn't even show this, all it reported of the entire ceremony was a news item with no picture

No breakfast, no lunch, now I can give myself a real treat: For the first time in my life, chestnut ice cream

What fantasy of concrete poetry could surpass this pastry menu:
Apple tart
Vanilla cream tart
French cream slice
Cream puff
Chocolate cream puff
Vienna cube
Cream flan
Pressburg nut crescent
Pressburg poppyseed crescent
Almond slice
Hollow wafer
Almond crescent
Chocolate torte
Dobosh torte

Goosefoot torte
Orange torte
Punch torte
Royal torte
Rosalinda torte
Sacher torte
Model torte
Chocolate torte à la mode
Dobosh torte à la mode
Fruit torte
Coffee cream torte
Chocolate punch dessert
King's bombe
Parisian bombe
Rococo dessert
Odessa dessert
Morning star
Rainbow
Giant potato
Nougat slice
Spike
Block
Brandy puff
Rigó-Jancsi dessert
Brazil dessert
Chocolate basket
Eve bombe
Mammoth roll
Little nightlight
Creole dessert
Strawberry puff
Coffee Ney dessert
Orange slice
Chestnut puff

Chestnut tunnel
Grillage shell
Chestnut basket
Strawberry basket
Raspberry basket
Artist
Mixed ice cream
Ice cup with whipped cream
Coffee with ice cream and whipped cream
Ice cream flambé
Parfait slice with whipped cream
Chestnut parfait
Punch parfait with chocolate sauce
Cabinet pudding with punch sauce
Dutch cube with chocolate sauce and whipped cream
Chocolate in glass
Chestnut cream
Fruit cream
Chestnut purée with whipped cream
Ice cream bombe
Nut-brittle bombe
Chocolate bombe
Mixed dessert
Cardinal Brandy
French Cognac
Grand Gin
Scotch Whisky
Lánchíd Cognac
Club 99 Whisky
Unicum
Hubertus
Cherry Brandy
Curaçao
Mocca Liqueur

Vermouth
Cinzano
Orange juice
Pineapple juice
Grapefruit juice
Coca Cola
Lemonade
Soda water
(the only thing not listed is coffee

Lánchíd – Chain Bridge. In Berlin we give an English pronunciation to the name of the cognac, a Lánchíd; how is
one to know that it is pronounced Laanzheet? Does the
taste of the cognac change with the pronunciation? Does
Lánchíd taste differently from Laanzheet? I would think
so

The black of Chain Bridge –cognac brown intensified to
the nth degree

Chain Bridge: mighty military emplacements; Roman for-
tresses; gateways; masses of iron like pieces of a fantastic
war machine, and the lions with vampire teeth and no
tongues

Massive iron candelabra, the feet solid and unpierced, the
casings fearsome dungeons, as if each evening the daylight
were imprisoned there

The much-derided tonguelessness keeps the lions slim

And again, more movie memories: Lang's *M*; I saw – I
was ten – a trailer of it and saw Peter Lorre's face staring

from the outer reaches of fear, always just the face looking at me as if I were the one who could understand and rescue it; I felt that this film would touch upon the secret of the grownups and couldn't understand why it was banned for children: whom else but children should a film about a child murder concern? I dreamed up a thousand desperate plans to get into the movie theater, somehow and unseen, but I believe I neither bawled nor begged (or am I just imagining that). ... Then my father told me the story of the movie the day after its first showing in Rochlitz, but that was nothing, that wasn't *M* and it wasn't that face staring out, and once again I learned that grownups were reluctant to yield their secrets and I asked no more, and it was shortly after that that I was sent to the monastery school

"M" as in mythology

Or *Dance on the Volcano*, that was in Reichenberg, when I went to every single showing, four times a day, as long as the film ran, which was two weeks, and I sat spellbound as during the first hour, waiting for the moment when Deburreau would tear off his clown's costume and I could hurl my hatred into the face of all the powers on earth with his frenzied hand; Cook the King a pottage that'll stick in his gullet and choke him to death

or when, that was in Reichenberg too, our high school senior class was herded by our P. T. teacher to see an educational movie on venereal diseases, how they are contracted, their consequences and their prevention; and we, an aura of blasé experience on our acne faces, sprawled nonchalantly beside the nonchalantly lounging co-eds, prepared not to turn a hair and yet to tremble and yet to find out. ... I remember sitting beside Milly and Axel, as we were waiting for the movie to start, even Axel wasn't smirking and Milly wasn't giggling; it was an expectant readiness, we were Hamlet, we were being treated as adults, I shall never forget that. ... There was a smell of newly whitewashed walls, the curtains did not close properly, the daylight was gray and clammy, like cold smoke; there was a long delay before the movie started, yet in spite of creaking chairs and subdued coughing there was complete silence until at last the beam of light started whirring and endless rows of pus-eroded sexual organs invaded Helsingör; it was not the ghost who appeared, it was right away Fortinbras who came marching in with regiments of scrota and vulval labis, glands and clitores; it must have been crazy, an orgy of abstrusity, we were dazed and increasingly bewildered. Then all the other parts of the body appeared, all encrusted and eroded with pus as if the creator of the film wanted to give a complete survey of everything in the human body that could be putrefied: eyes, finger joints, breasts, groins, upper lips, lower lips, corners of the mouth, roof of the mouth, tongue, tip of the tongue, gums, chin, dimple, jaws, auricle, ear lobe, it was German and thorough and complete, bulldozing all thinking, feeling and wanting, German sex instruction, German anti-porn, an orgy of gracelessness. Melodramatic as it may sound today, we might have emerged from this movie transformed, for we all felt for the first time that we were being taken seriously and as adults; but as it was we sank in despair into leaden apathy, and if there was one thing of which we were sure it was that never again did we want to have any more sex instruction. This time, of course, the little daytime whores who were lying in wait for us, expecting eager customers, were out of luck; I wondered whether they could sue for loss of business, but in the end they dragged off the P. T. teacher

But then in Poltava, when Hans-Joachim R., the general's son, undressed in his quarters the evening he arrived and drew his fingernails across the yellow skin under his breast, saying off-handedly: "Wherever I squeeze my flesh, pus comes out, I'm all pus, you know," we stared at him in speechless admiration; although he was a puny, lazy weakling, he was accepted by wordless concensus as our leader; he made plans for grandiose projects, among others for a distillery and private reconnaissance actions into the mystery-shrouded, forbidden suburb, but he accomplished none of it, as soon after that he was blown up by partisans on a leave-train; that, too, is a bit of Fascism which I have intended to write about ten times and at which I have failed ten times

Chain Bridge: a harp with strings of angle iron; who plays it

Hard-currency store for arts and crafts; in the window, a lot of art nouveau vases; two slim youths, leather jackets, blue jeans, stand at the window, conversing in under-tones; they smooth down their hair with spit, take a deep breath, and resolutely walk in

Something that never ceases to amaze me: this close re-lationship between logic and fairy tale. It is a mark of the fairy tale that everything can communicate with everything and everyone with everyone, but that is also a mark of logic! I can express the universe and any object I like and any situation in it I like by any other object I like or any other situation I like, let's say: the Andromeda nebula by an orange blossom – all I need is to form a true statement with "orange blossom," for instance: "Every orange blossom smells of caravans," and I can then reshape this sentence as follows: "Everything in the universe either smells of caravans or is not an orange blossom," and that also applies to the Andromeda nebula, thus: "The Andromeda nebula either smells of caravans, or it is not an orange blossom

Poetry cannot necessarily do this (nor can myth), its logic is stricter than that of logistic. Without further substantiation, it could only put Orion together with the orange blossom

The world can be expressed by poetry because it can be mathematized

With Zoltán in a tiny movie house way out, even beyond the suburbs, even beyond the clay pits. *Sparkling Winds*, a film about social problems in 1947, i.e., a historical film, but rendered alien by today's costumes (blue jeans, sweaters) and by the props and rites of Mao followers. Zoltán translates; I understand everything and understand nothing. On our way home Zoltán explains the historical situation, and now I would like to see the film once more, but it won't be shown again

And in the store right next to the little movie house – Hungarian salami which hasn't been available in the big stores in Budapest all this time! I turn to Zoltán, who knows all there is to know about Hungary, for the secret of this salami manufacture, but all he says is: "It's special meat, special smoke, special spices and special drying," then he grins and says no more

The ride through the night on the open streetcar platform; the long ride in the blue dark, and the little lights along the way, and the awareness of the Danube and the cool stream of air, and the long, detailed conversation without any misgivings

"Able to say anything" – one must examine each of the three completely different sentences resulting from change of emphasis, and hear how in the negation the "not" moves through these sentences like the rustling wings of the angel of death

At night the desire to listen to the radio, and now I do have a splendid set, and it lights up, it even gets warm, but then all it produces is a hum, a hum like a ghost of music – a symbol of what, for Heaven's sake, is that supposed to be

The monastery-school boys in *Sparkling Winds* all seem so strangely alien to me. Was I like that too? Suddenly everything is open to doubt

What happened to me in Kalksburg was a change too, and what a change: I entered as a naively pious, deeply religious, God-fearing child, and four years later I ran away a convinced atheist: black box, input and output

The dialectics of pedagogy; that infinitely stupid, misanthropic statement: "A schoolboy's head contains only that which we put into it

Can there really be changes against one's will? Certainly: the change in Kalksburg happened against my will. And unnoticed changes? Oh yes. Imagined changes? Those too.

And changes which, though willed, lead to a different result from the willed one? And can one really *will* changes,
don't they just happen to one

Resolution for Berlin: Aristoteles

October 27

Dream:
I am sitting in a plane and know that I am flying to
Finland. Vague impression of passengers, many
men, children too; next to me a young woman;
I don't know anybody. No clouds, no landscape,
perhaps no windows. The interior of the aircraft
resembles a kitchen; instead of the pilot's cabin a
kitchen closet; on the right, dirty dishes in the sink;
on the left a refrigerator; beyond, dimly, several
tiers of bunks. We land; it is the middle of the night;
we are on the top of a hill, and although it is
completely dark I know we are on that Thessalian
hill where in September 1944 we lay for five days
in our tent in pouring rain. We get out; dry ground;
piles of hay; we feel the hay and lie down in it. I fall
asleep immediately. Dawn; a whistle; we wake up,
the plane has gone. It is no longer pitch-dark but still
very dark. We crawl aimlessly around the slope
of the hill, looking for the plane; close up, I recognize
one or two of the faces, including that of my neighbor.
Low woods; we search and search; here and there
the beam of a flashlight, but we cannot find the
plane. Suddenly I remember that I have left my
money in my briefcase on the plane; I am alarmed,
and just then, some way off, I see a very steep
sugar-loaf mountain and the plane standing on its
flattened top. Now the others have seen it too, and
we at once start to climb the steep slope of the sugar
loaf, in a closely packed group, holding onto the
grass and pulling ourselves up. The climb is
laborious, and I wonder why one doesn't lose weight
in one's sleep after such efforts, when suddenly

a wave of grass divides, a tall woman of about forty
rising up from it. She has been defecating; she
stands in profile to us, her knees still slightly bent,
her underpants down and her buttocks smeared
with excrement. She looks at us in consternation,
then, without wiping, she pulls up her panties and
disappears in the grass, and a young man in front
of me collapses into the grass, groaning: My god!
That at last! and he looks up rapturously at the sky,
and I know: he will stay right there and never see
Finland.

We have reached the plane and board it, when a
huge mastiff leaps out at us from one of the bunks,
shakes itself and stares at us, but no one is afraid; we
shove it to one side when we want to pass, and it puts
up with this treatment although it sometimes growls
and paws the ground. The plane is already airborne;
once again gray, no clouds, no view. I feel hungry
and go to the refrigerator and open the door and
see a gnome crouching in the back left corner in the
otherwise empty, icicle-glittering space. With a start
I slam the door shut, but one of the passengers, a
quiet elderly man, says: Why don't you let the poor
fellow out, he'll freeze to death in there! I nod in
embarrassment and open the door, and the gnome
crawls out. He reminds me of little round S. Müller,
who seemed to be put together of little round balls
and who went to school with B.; I address him in
Russian and he replies in German, which surprises
me greatly. I say: We are flying to Finland! and the
gnome looks at me for a moment in disgust, then
he dashes past me toward a bowl of tomatoes
standing on the kitchen shelf, snatches it up, gobbles
up some tomatoes, and says through his chewing

and gulping: I am a famous nigger-killer! Cries of
annoyance, of horror. The gnome puffs out his chest,
but the man who had interceded for him darts
forward and slaps him. At this the gnome covers
his face with his hands; he actually shrinks still
further; his body emanates an icy hatred; I shudder,
but I grab the gnome by the collar and shut him up
again in the refrigerator. That's not enough! says
the man, and shuts in the mastiff as well. I am about
to protest but am reassured by the thought that the
mastiff is harmless and that it can keep the gnome
company. Yet hardly has the refrigerator been
closed again when the sound of banging and
hammering and howling comes from inside it; it is
a desperate, heart-rending howl; as we stand
helplessly around the refrigerator, an old woman
speaks up: The little chap's hungry, why don't you
give him something! She takes the bowl of tomatoes
and pushes it through the wall of the refrigerator
to the gnome, and the hammering and howling
cease immediately. The plane lands again, but this
time we spend the night on board; in the morning
there is again a whistle, and as the plane rises I see
that some of the passengers, including the woman
who had been sitting next to me and the man who
slapped the gnome, have disappeared. The
refrigerator is silent. I open the door, peer in and see
the gnome lying bound between the feet of a lion,
into which the mastiff had presumably been
transformed. The lion opens his jaws wide; I stick
in my head and pull it out again after a long while,
glancing at the gnome as I do so. His eyes are closed,
yet through the lids I sense his icy hatred and,
satisfied, I quickly close the refrigerator door.

But already we are landing again; we get out; we are standing on a street in some garden suburb, and I know we are in Weimar. I would like to phone Ursula but can't find a telephone booth and go for a walk. On the way I have to step over straw wreaths lying about on the street; it amuses me to hop over them, and soon I am hopping over fences and houses, and at last I discover a telephone booth and hop inside, and on opening the door I find the gnome sitting inside, wagging his head and saying: I'm going to kill you soon, you just wait! I slam the door shut and hop away in panic. Empty field; stubble; piles of straw; no plane; I am alone, and down there lies Weimar. I hop down and arrive in a large, tiled, underground room, a very high, very light, very pleasant large room with tiled walls and beds, a cross between a military hospital and a spa. I am twenty-five. Many people about, men and women, most of them in swimsuits, some in hospital gowns or pajamas, here and there nurses with caps and milky white skin. A fruit vendor walks through the crowd selling little bags of cherries and plums from his tray; I buy some plums from him and flick away the stones, and one of them hits a young, rather exotic-looking man in a bathrobe who is sitting beside a girl, also in a bathrobe, on a bench without a back. I call out an apology; but he laughs good-naturedly and says: Why don't you come for a shower with us? I nod, and join them; he shakes my hand, so does the girl, then they throw off their bathrobes, but their bodies are so indistinct that I can't see whether they are naked or clothed. I myself am now wearing swim trunks. We go into the shower room; the couple step under the shower and put their heads together; their hair flows together, it has a bluish sheen. I make for a vacant shower, but the young man calls out: Come on in here! I join them; the girl shakes out her hair, and she is standing there naked; she is completely at ease and enjoys the shower and displays her body shining with water. I have laid my head on the young man's shoulder and look at the girl with profound pleasure and total absence of desire. She is extremely beautiful, fresh, firm, maybe twenty years old, the skin a pale golden brown, the eyes very slightly slanted, and from her breasts across her belly down to her genital area and framing her pubic hair waves a half-inch line of thick black hair like the horse's tail on a Greek helmet. It is the highest perfection of physical beauty I have ever seen; it is grace in unfettered freedom, and I would like to stand there for hours, just looking, and she notices it and stands motionless under the running water. Now she smiles, and now I know for sure that she is Mongolian, and I also see that the young man, who now turns his head to look at me, is a Mongolian. His complexion is golden-brown, his hair blue-black, the eyes are slanted. I say: You're a Mongolian, aren't you? He nods, and now his eyes rest on me, and I sense in them a strange coldness, and he says softly: I am, and you'll soon find out what's inside a Mongolian

After this dream, feelings of fear, violent palpitations, piercing headache behind my forehead

Libraries; Prof. D.; then B. B., "blissful Blasius

Between Gerbeaud's and the city park, the old Metro, the first subway station in Europe, a real streetcar under ground, seventy years old and as true to that time as a picture by Henri Rousseau or a verse by Apollinaire. Two little cars like wedding coaches, two plump gondolas, two merry-go-round boats moving straight ahead, two jolly Charon's arks, two chaises for market women, two elongated equipages, two horseless charabancs for under-ground outings, two skiffs on wheels with planks for sitting inside around the bow and the stern, and in the middle, hanging down from the roof, thirty-one loops in eleven rows, like thirty-one handshakes from the Metro admin-istration

Everything that moves from the equator toward the poles becomes a little bit heavier; I believe that every-thing that boards this Metro becomes a little bit friend-lier

The loops shake hands with each other

Yesterday the movie was a minor carnival; many young people who I am sure understood little of its problematics, but then they weren't looking for a lesson in philosophy or history. They joined in the performance with loud com-ments and had a marvelous time, and so they should: one of the leading figures challenged the monastery-school stu-dents to a discussion, and when he formulated the first question: "What role does personality play in history?" and the students remained obstinately silent, the reply came from the audience. "None at all!" a bass voice called out from the front row, and everyone laughed and every-thing was clear

Another loud comment was addressed to a bigoted female character. "Oh cut it out! I bet you'd like a good fuck with the priest!" someone called out, and it sounded like kindly advice. "No, not her!" replied a voice from another row, and: "Sure, sure!" others called out vehemently. "For Chrissake," said the bass up front, "that broad?" and the reply shot back: "Sure, that broad!" It was all good fun among experts, and from the screen the heroine was calling: "The sparkling winds blow ahead

In the newsreel, scenes from a little Hungarian town: under a sign identifying a building as a home for girls – the building was of imposing dimensions – there was also a sign indicating the maternity ward and the abortion commission. Needless to say, that prompted roars of laughter too, and again hearty and unaffected; but, as Zoltán told me later, and as I had heard from others, a high-school girl becoming pregnant still constitutes a tragedy, entailing expulsion from school, paternal execration, and being cast out of the parental home

In the bus, a breakneck ride across Chain Bridge, beyond the bridge an abrupt swerve and, with undiminished speed, around the hairpin bend of a detour. ... At yesterday's movie, the jeep-chase shown in the trailer was nothing, the Budapest buses can do better. ... The most remarkable thing is the passengers who remain calmly on their feet while the foreigner is flung from one corner to the other. They must have their center of gravity somewhere in their calves

This time with Ferenc: the film version of Brook's *Marat/Sade* production: as a document, interesting; as a film, we felt, a total failure

With Zoltán, continuing the conversation about 1956. ...
"The most terrible thing for which Rákosi was respon-
sible," says Zoltán, "was the apathy of the population. No
one was interested any more in what the Party had to say,
it could have said whatever it liked, people just nodded
to everything and said mechanically: Sure, that's right!,
loud and clear and quite mechanically: Sure, that's right!
and they nodded at the greatest falsehoods, and those
idiots proclaimed this as a victory, and meanwhile not
even their most obvious truths were believed

Zoltán's favorite epithet (value-free): "foxy": "a foxy fellow" – "a foxy speaker" – "as foxy as a Kashow lawyer"

Zoltán: "The hardest part was to get into a dialogue again
with the population; all dialogue with it had ceased. If
only one person speaks and merely wants to hear confirmation from the other of what he has said, that's no longer a
dialogue, and soon after people even stop listening

In the evening, a reading in a small circle; a discussion
develops on the mass-deportation of Germans after the
end of the war. My approval arouses protest, to my utter
consternation.
    Such a reaction is a sign of provincialism: being unable
to envisage the possibility of any view other than one's own,
at least not among friends. Essentially this is another form
of national arrogance – the very thing I find so repellent

The protest triggered a discussion; each has defended his
position – and now what? Has the debate been pointless
because no one has convinced anyone else? Not at all:
I have a chance to examine and confirm my point of view
(how my opponent fared I don't know), I have enlarged

my knowledge, and both are worth-while. A muscle that is not used wastes away

The hotel porter had promised to send a mechanic for my radio, but nothing

Nagyon fáj – finished in rough draft; a lovely poem by Gábor:

Encouraging Myself

Before you enter the mists
just utter just utter what is yours
before you enter the mists
speak for your dead friends
before you enter the mists
speak of starvation of shivering of fear
before you enter the mists
speak of the shame of centuries
before you enter the mists
speak of the shame of your dead forefathers
before you enter the mists
stiffen your neck ever stiffer
before you enter the mists
just utter just utter the curses of the tortured

before you enter the mists
for you are bound to enter the mists

Rereading the poem I hear familiar voices: "What's the allusion here, what does this H. mean with his mists, surely not the natural phenomenon!" – "Of course not," I reply, "by mists he means whatever are for you, the reader, the mists!" – "I see," say the voices, "so what are these mists really?" – "They are what you are bound to enter," I reply

The mists: for me they are becoming more and more my own self, my own past

"The water has brought you; the foam has swept you here!"

Can't get to sleep. To amuse myself, draw up rules and regulations for J. J.'s proposed "Society for Mutual Admiration". ... It would have to be organized in sections, of course, more specifically sections headed "those who": section of those who teach, section of those who write, section of those who command, section of those who lead, section of those who judge, section of those who answer, section of those who direct the economy, section of those who practice sports, and so on; the heads of each section in turn form a further section, the section of those who admire, with a president, two vice-presidents, a business manager and, in charge of trainees, the Director of the Institute for Admiration. Monthly meetings of each section with admiration of each member in turn; joint annual conference with papers on the theory and practice of admiring (suggestions: The Advanced Development of True Aesthetics by Widespread Expansion of Admiring; Against Formalism in the "Production" of Some "Admirers"; Toward Work Productivity by Systematic Admiration of General Managements; Information? No, Admiration!; The Emergence of Characteristics of Collective Admiration in the Developed Primal Community; New Masterpieces in Epic Writing on Admiration; Our Admirers are Life-Affirming!); plus an annual banquet with the awarding of three prizes each for outstanding examples of admiration in the fields of poetry, journalism, the arts, music and drama, as well as every three years a special prize for Positive Satire and Criticism

October 28

With Zoltán to Szeged; preceded by lengthy wavering between whether to go Trans- or Cis-Danubia, to Pécs or Szeged, to history or Germanistics, and in the end the earlier train decided for us

Clear, fresh day, a foxy morning, to use Zoltán's word; up early; a few exercises, a bit of grammar, and now off in high spirits to the River Tisza

With its glass paneling the Western Station borders directly on the Great Ring; from the street you can watch the workaday routine of the locomotives like a window display; you can see soundless snorting and rattling and whistling and hissing and crashing of bumpers and screeching of steel on steel and cries of mothers and chuffing of electric carts and tramping and gabbling and hurrying and shouting; a pantomime of noise, just like a dream and in all its aspects as if staged by a genie

On one occasion, though, a locomotive crashed through the glass wall onto the sidewalk and murdered five of the onlookers

Clouds like little cherubs' little buttocks

Public services in a show window, I can only remember seeing this with menders or stocking repairers; it is something that should be extended beyond workshops: to public offices, courts, schools, prisons

The trains depart with no boarding signal – like people leaving a party without saying good-bye

Zoltán is having a snack: four fried eggs, in sizzling lard of course, with thick slices of white bread of course, and with it a triple *barackpálinka* since we are soon to be traveling through apricot country

Bare acacia groves outside

Endless, harvested maize fields alternate with endless fields of frosted cabbage, between them rows of bare poplars fluttering their last leaves, and at intervals of many kilometers here and there some white farm buildings

The dream about the Mongolians still hangs over me. ... Strange, in the dream I had the feeling of bliss such as I had never experienced, of a crystalline enchantment of pure loveliness, and what has remained is the oppressive feeling I had on waking, the threat in those mysterious words: You'll soon find out what's inside a Mongolian

Screaming seagulls, but that's impossible, where would they come from in the plains

Vines: growing on the flat plain; it looks so strange, I had always thought of vines growing on slopes

Endless orchards of little chest-high trees, the famous apricots of Kecskemét, the picker needs no ladder or special tools. The little trees have hardly any trunk; the tops spread out a few hand-breadths above the ground; the tops above, the roots below, the trunk is indeed superfluous: basic equipment for a tree, no: a fruit tree. Again no: in the forests near Berlin, in the tree farms, they grow fir trees no taller than a man

The berry bushes, were they once trees? Design, let's say, a gooseberry tree

Seen from the train, the crowns of the trees really do look like crowns

Lonely, whitewashed farm buildings; thatched roofs; draw wells; the plains, the *puszta* just as you imagined it and, prompted by the isolated farms, Zoltán gives me a private lesson on Hungarian history

Zoltán: You people don't know what it means to have feared three times in history for the existence of the Hungarian people and language, to have been confronted three times by national extermination: with the physical liquidation by the Tatars in the thirteenth century, enslavement by the Turks in the sixteenth, and being pulverized between Slavs and Germans in the seventeenth and eighteenth centuries

"Among Slavs, Germans, Vlachs and other peoples, the Hungarians now form the lesser part of the population, and centuries hence there may be hardly a trace of their language to be found."
  According to Zoltán, this gloomy prognosis, formulated about 1780, is known to every Hungarian, and it occurs in one of the profoundest and most humane works of that time, *Ideas on the Philosophy of the History of Mankind*, and is known simply as "Herder's prophecy

Not: disintegration, internal feuds, pauperization, loss of statehood, suppression, loss of culture, no: fear for sheer ethnic survival

Ah, who is there to praise the Cumans, who perished, the almond-eyed, intrepid Cumans, crazed by their thirst for liberty. ... A few names recall them, a few fantastic landmarks in Magyar history, but they themselves are no more: slain by the sword, the ax, by arrows, burned to death, torn apart by dogs, starved to death, hanged, suffocated in bogs, flayed, dragged to death

No, we don't know what it means, and there is no way we can duplicate those emotions

As for the German defeats, since, with the exception of World War I, there were always Germans on both sides, they had no life-threatening consequences for the nation; in fact some, like that of 1806, were from certain aspects what May 1945 was in totality: a historical gain as a possibility for radical democratization. The victories on the other hand, the victories, the victories

It is strange: although as a soldier I was, in both purpose and consciousness, an unquestioning believer in Hitler, yet I was apprehensive of victory, or more correctly: I dreaded it – even more, of course, and in a different sense, defeat. The perspective of victory was an unending, dreary soldier's existence somewhere in the Urals; the perspective of defeat seemed tantamount to ethnic annihilation. What grew out of this pair of alternatives was the saying, terrible in itself yet accurately expressing a mass mood: "Enjoy the war, comrades, peace will be terrible!" It has been forgotten

So perhaps we can share those feelings? Far from it. What for me was a chimera was for the Hungarians three times a reality. It is the difference between imagination and experience, between fantasy and reality

(Phrases such as: "Imagination was worse than reality," or vice versa, are false. Imagination is inherently different from reality

The fate which the Tatars tried to impose on the vanquished can only be compared with the "final solution to the Jewish problem." It was genocide, even the methods were essentially the same: after military occupation, pogrom and slaughtering of able-bodied men; a gleam of hope, prompting those who had fled or hidden to reveal themselves and reassemble; euphoric affliction; ghettoization; summonses to report; mass roundups; selections; transportation; seizing of all possessions. Liquidation. The Latin report of an eyewitness, that of Rogerius, has been preserved; it should be translated and published, it is a European document

(From Roger's report: "One year of Tatar rule had totally laid waste the country. Administration and the judicial system had collapsed, the army pulverized, almost all the able-bodied men wiped out. In many areas, not a single living soul was to be found in journeys of two or three days."

At that time Pope and Emperor, the seventh Gregory and the fourth Henry, were fighting for supremacy. Each called himself the protector of Christianity, each was aware of Hungary's agony from detailed reports, each could have helped, yet each regarded the other as the greater peril. Even so, for Füst, Henry IV was a banner:

"... that here once lived my Henry, the King, that here
        once bled his heart,
Who remains to bear witness? And here was also I –
        for me to be a last trumpet with which to blast
So that somewhere his piteous bones may quake."

The Turks who followed were almost tolerant, they were content to enslave and were probably keener on assimilation by conversion than on outright annihilation

The Janissaries, the Turks' Praetorian guard, were re cruited exclusively from Christian youths who had con verted to Islam; great literary documents of the will to Islamization are said to exist, but we know nothing of all that

Zoltán: "When the Beys and the Pashas were riding around here, we groveled, we groveled down under the grass, groveled in the stickiest mud, groveled in the blackest shame, we ate grass and we ate dust, but we survived and our language persisted

Zoltán: "You still hear people say: The black brew is yet to come! When a Hungarian was invited by a Turk, i.e., one of his masters, he was courteously received and graciously served; during the meal only pleasant topics were discussed, but then came the coffee, and then the master came to the point, and the point was even more bitter than the black coffee

"And 'Cruciturks'!" says Zoltán, "the expletive 'Cruciturks'! – that's another reminder of the Turkish era, a contraction of 'crucifix' and 'Turks' enabling the reactionaries to equate the inner foe with the hated foreign enemy, a proven method

"The noonday bells," says Zoltán, "also originated in the Turkish period: when Hunyádi János was victorious at Belgrade, bells rang out all over Europe

And after Prince Eugene's great victory, the bells of Christendom rang out again. That was the second battle near the city-fortress of Belgrade; by that time the Turks had already been beaten at Mohács, and there were also two battles of Mohács: in 1526 the decisive, disastrous defeat at the hands of the Turks, and in 1687 the liberating victory. It is significant that only the first battle of Mohács has remained alive in memory, and I venture to say that this phenomenon denotes the Hungarians' awareness that it was this mortal threat which gave the impetus to their powers of resuscitation

Yet probably the poets of no other nation have dealt as mercilessly with their own people as have the poets of Hungary with the nation that twice saved Europe. ... A volume of national self-criticism in various languages would be a most useful and interesting anthology, and it should be headed by the following:

Ady Endre: *We Need Mohács*

> If God there be, no mercy must He show him:
> He's used to being beaten,
> Faint-hearted scion of the gypsy people,
> Just beat him, beat him, beat him.
>
> If God there be, no pity must He show me:
> I am a native Magyar.
> His sacred dove no olive branch must carry,
> Just hit me, flog me, flog me.
>
> If God there be, drag us He must
> From earth to shining sky.
> No respite should we have, not half a minute,
> For then we're finished, finished.

On the other hand, it would be hard to find many nations that have as intimate a relationship with their writers as do the Hungarians

Later, at the Institute, Prof. H. opens a volume of Babits, apparently at random, and I read: "This constant self-reproach, this self-goading, springs from inner necessity, from the conscience. This is what distinguishes it from the rhetoric of other nations. Hungarian speech is not a form of intellectual gymnastics, like French; nor is it the pathos of words, like Latin. Great Hungarian speech is emphatically not based on reason, even less is it a sensual indulgence, it is the solemn word of the conscience. ..."

At home, reread Engels' essays on the Hungarians in 1848; as I recall, they are among the most beautiful things ever said about Hungary in the German language

In making his prognosis, Herder had in mind the fate of the vanished Baltic peoples, the Kurs and the Pruzzes; a warning example that it is inadmissible to draw analogy conclusions in history

Bobrowski's poetry is a fine example of what it means to "fulfill one's partial function." I must confess that my first reaction to his poetry was one of sharp rejection, in fact I saw in it something impermissible: the keeping awake, perhaps even the reawakening, of feelings that were bound to die out, sentiments evoked by the memories of misty mornings beyond the Vistula and the sweet call of the oriole. ... I had a concept of overcoming the past which, while honorable enough, was very narrow, and I even choked off my own song. But there is no deleting from history, not a single aspect and not a single emotion, they can only be canceled out in the Hegelian sense. Not a "It never happened," nor a "As if it had never happened," but only a "That's the way it was, and it is past" is the secure foundation on which to build something new

Another aspect of the same thing: finally get away from mutual buttering up, be frank in our opinions, even in public, take each other seriously

What we can learn from Hungary's history, Hungary's literature: the power of ruthless self-criticism, the combination of truth and dignity; openness to the world as the self-image of a small nation, to preserve itself from the threat of inundation not by encapsulating itself (which would be either impossible or crippling), but by raising itself to the level of world culture

Zoltán grew up speaking three languages: Hungarian, German, Slovak (and Yiddish too, if you like); he speaks all these languages, plus French, without an accent, can communicate in Russian, Serbian, English, Czech, Polish, Italian, and he also reads Latin. Every educated Hungarian speaks at least two foreign languages, most of them speak three or four, and well enough to be able to read philosophy or poetry in them, and in addition they read Latin, and often Greek. The Hungarian translation-culture, in terms of quantity and quality, is admirable; it is taken for granted that any Hungarian poet is capable of recreating poems from another language, and when on one occasion I praised a Hungarian translation of Goethe's *Pandora* with the remark that, taking the rhythm and intonation of any given passage, it is possible to quote the corresponding German line, I was met with the amazed reply: But of course, that's what is expected

Wittgenstein's terrible words: The limits of my language
represent the limits of my world

"So then the Prince walked up and down the streets, saw
many wondrously clothed and comely persons and tried in
twenty-seven languages – that is, as many languages as the
Prince could speak – to converse with them, but no one
responded. That saddened him. What was he to do here
if he could not speak to anyone! Much downcast he walked
up and down until he suddenly caught sight of a man wearing the garments customary in his own land. ..."

And naturally his countryman speaks the language of
that realm: it is the Realm of the Blue King and lies at the
end of the world. ... The prince of many tongues – a
feature of the Hungarian fairy tale which I cannot remember having come across in the fairy tales of other nations

Because of its arcades, the cathedral square of Szeged is
a pantheon of Hungarian culture and history; this would
be a good spot from which to look north. And what do you
see first? This: that the German nation has actually turned
into a historical concept. In spite of its foreign language
you feel attached to Hungary, in spite of sharing the same
language you feel separated from that other German state.
And second: the people of the German Democratic Republic are no longer a nation of eighty million people; we
have become a small nation burdened by the heavy obliga-
tions of a special position: that of having a language of
world status. It behooves us to remember our tradition, but
as an obligation, not as a credential

Zoltán warned me that Szeged is not what you might call
a beautiful city: apart from the Church of the Franciscans
hardly an ancient stone – the great flood, he said, had

swept almost everything away, and in its wake a Hapsburg provincial drawing-board capital had arisen, devoid of imagination, inorganic, monotonous, pseudo-historic – oh well, he may be right, it may all be true, but it is and always will be the city of Radnóti

and from the trees hang foot-long blackish-brown pods in clusters; never have I seen anything like it, and Zoltán tells me it is a swamp plane tree which only grows here, you see

and around the Church of the Franciscans a triple belt of roses, and that *is* Saint Francis

and on the road out to the university a farm cart approaches us, laden with paprikas, great pods in wreaths, an explosion of red, one little horse is brown, one little horse is white, the driver is black, and beside the cart, weaving and bottle-green under the swaying pods, a group of young fellows singing at the top of their voices:

> A cold wind blows
> Mother, bring me my cape
> Tonight I am going to my old love

and from all the windows snow-white women look down, and on the fruit stalls lie little gray fruits that I don't know, and the statue of the famous Dankó Pista allows even sparrows to swarm around it, and a whiff of charcoal smoke is wafted through the leafy autumn air

Szőke Tisza, the blonde River Tisza, the bent elbow of the *puszta*

While here, have another go at Ady

Yellow-brown world; brownish-yellow shallow water, pale yellow-brown river bank, crumbling loess, and silvery-green willow shrubs, trunkless and silvery-green in pale brown, and above, yellow, the last of the poplar leaves, and the blue sky, and the smell of fish

The river bank is deeply fissured, low and fissured, steps, terraces, tiers, caves, gemlike in wide ovals

And flatboats, sand barges, ferry boats, oval lighters on their way south, smoke-blackened, likewise brown and yellow, and the pale-yellow loads of sand

Two gray screaming pigeons flapping in descent, they almost plummet, land with a jolt, stagger, and immediately go for each other

You couldn't picture the Danube in a storm, but you can visualize the Tisza in flood, yellow gurgling waves, water full of loess rising as it races along and spilling over the embankment and washing the city into the *puszta* and trickling away with it

At the Germanistic Institute, a visit to Professor Halász, the author of the famous dictionary that Ilona calls a miracle (which it is) – what is it that makes this atmosphere, like all the rest of intellectual Hungary, so pleasant? Absolute openness of speech is the rule of the game, and that even includes ruthlessness, even callousness, even spite, but it is taken for granted that one's opponent can defend himself, and no third element is involved in this defense or attack, at least nothing outside the cultural sphere

Well, no doubt touchiness too, hurt feelings, groups and cliques and certainly intrigues, but – and this is the point –

as ingredients of intellectual freedom of movement, not as a barrier to it, and hence no objection to them

It is very odd, but we have got into the habit of accepting a necessary attribute of a given entity as reason to exclude it instead of learning to see its positive aspects. Thus we have sought, for instance, to reduce abstract art *ad absurdum* by – and this can be done – laboriously proving that it is not concrete, instead of exploring its possibilities as a transitional phase. Or we say about an opinion: "But that's so subjective!" believing that we have offered a devastating argument against that opinion, instead of starting from the premise that an opinion, if it wishes to transcend the established objective level of knowledge to arrive at new insights, or new aspects, or even only new arguments, is bound to be subjective

("Yes, sure, 'subjective' of course, but not *that* subjective

Wonder whether others have also found that intolerant people are very partial to dirty jokes

In the seminar a discussion on whether it is possible to recreate poems from languages that one does not speak at all or only very little. It seems futile to try and persuade a Hungarian that one can even embark on such an enterprise. Yet it is precisely here that a true collaboration is possible, for translating a poem is a matter not of two languages but of three: of the source language, the target language, and the universal language of poetry. A Hungarian poem is not simply "Hungarian," it is Hungarian and it is a poem; and when the Hungarian has been translated into German, the second translation, the one within the German language, still remains to be done; and if someone attempts this who does not understand the language of poetry, the first translation is usually destroyed too. ... It then becomes a kind of pidgin-poetry with the characteristics of pidgin-German. ...

No, in spite of the phenomenon that these languages appear in the linguistic form of only two, a true division of labor between the interlinear translator and the re-creator (not a very good word but I can't find a better one) is possible and in certain cases, particularly in dealing with the languages of small nations, positively indicated. It was a bold move, but it paid off, and it succeeded: a dogma of the theory and practice of translation has been overturned. We actually entered upon virgin soil here, exploiting the potential of socialist publishing, but all this makes scarcely any impression

When modern grammarians examine the origin of what they call "well-formed sentences," and appoint a "competent speaker" to decide what represents a well-formed sentence in a given natural language, they (or their "competent speaker") extract from common usage something that might be called "poetic language in its total potential." This, of course, constitutes no objection to generative grammar, just as the term "poetic language" is not to be interpreted in a purely popular-romantic sense ("Beautiful!" "So poetic!" "How heart-warming!" "That's real art!" and so on). A *lingua poetica* of that kind may also contain grammatically incorrect and even completely senseless phrases, such as: "Cluck yourself clucker!" from Brecht's *Simone*

In that case the interlinear translator would be the "competent speaker" of the source language and the target language, the recreator (form-giver?) would be the "competent speaker" for the target and the poetic language

The relationship which the three languages enter during the process of translation can be expressed in the form of a syllogism, a conclusion from the *Dimatis* figure

Another amusing definition: the realm of the poetic is what lies beyond the well-formed sentences

The accomplishment of transposing two words in a given sentence can be greater than the translation of that same sentence from the source to the target language

Karl Kraus never wearied of pointing out that the transposition of two words, the replacement of one adjective by another of similar meaning, even the altering of a single prefix or of the punctuation, can transform a great poem into an amorphous (slick, trivial, dead, empty) structure, a non-poem ("a great harebell" – "a dainty harebell"; "come, ye quickly joyful!" – "come ye, quickly, joyful!") – and he is right

Form, in particular, is international in poetry. This thesis is the most baffling to the layman; he imagines it to be an insurmountable obstacle to recreating on the basis of a verbatim translation. But where a Hungarian or a German or an Albanian sonnet agree is in the sonnet form. I don't need to know a single word of Hungarian or Albanian to see (or better still: read) that I have a sonnet before me; and with a bit of practice I can even pinpoint difficult forms (the greatest feather in my cap: recognizing the antique, though varied, form of a Radnóti poem that Hungarian friends have described as being in free verse

Essential, however: a knowledge of stress, pronunciation, and the conception of rhyme. A comparative study of

rhymes would, incidentally, be a fascinating contribution
to the psychology of peoples

By my work in poetry translation I have fulfilled my partial function. As I have in children's literature. The third
(which ought really to be the first) got bogged down in the
first attempts

A late lunch with Professor Halász and Dottores P. and
K. (just for fun they are speaking Italian because they have
"the poorest command" of it) at a famous Szeged restaurant for the famous Szeged fish soup which, unlike the
familiar one, has to be creamy: first a broth of small fishes
is prepared and passed through a sieve, and in this broth
the carp is simmered

and of course this reminds you of that famous Roman dish:
the olive in the nightingale in the pigeon in the chicken in
the duck in the hare in the capon in the lamb in the deer
in the calf in the wild boar in the ox on the spit, with finally
only the olive being served, saturated with all the juices,
essence to the twelfth degree, and I feel that there is something eminently Hungarian about this

In the evening a long walk with Zoltán, night-blue sky, the
smell of charcoal, the smell of fish, the smell of acacias,
from tall chimneys white smoke. We walk through empty
streets, a desolate area near the port, when suddenly Zoltán grabs my arm, drags me over to a ruined wall, skims
up it like a cat, and pulls me up after him. I follow him;
I have no idea what it's all about. "Quick!" says Zoltán,
and I jump down, and we hurry in through the shadows
of a factory yard, when from the direction of the port
comes the sound of trotting and scraping, interspersed with

the clicking of hard hooves, blatting and bleating and a strangely wistful howling snort, a lamentation on dewlaps and nostrils, and as we squeeze into a recess four black-robed men appear, like herdsmen in their dress and demeanor, but black; with black military caps and black flapping coats and great black crooks with which they tap the ground at every step; as they walk along, tapping, they slowly turn their heads and peer into every corner, and Zoltán squeezes my hand and I understand and hold my breath. ... But the tapping men do not look into our recess; their gaze passes over us like a cold draft; they withdraw, and we cautiously lean forward and see a shepherd boy, barefoot in his white knee-length cotton smock, he passes, white against the sky, all in profile, Cuman-eyed, Cuman-sad, and now the trampling becomes louder and so does the tapping of the staves, and at that moment, invisible in the sky, music starts, a Danube waltz, sobbing violins, and soundlessly in the gliding of the waltz and soundlessly bleating and munching, there enter, at the very end of the yard, cheek by jowl into the strange milky light, their bodies becoming fully visible on the long straight path: little donkeys, six of them, two zebras, and, with an immensely long neck and frisky head and prancing a llama, and tufted, desert-yellow, four camels, led with nose-rings by youths, and at the end of the procession, its plump striped neck garlanded in green, an okapi, Op art from the Congo, and the little herd trots along in a willing pack, with lowered heads, and while the music swells and black herdsmen bring up the rear of the procession, a sudden gust of wind presses down the white smoke from the chimneys, a dry, curling, milky-transparent smoke into the nostrils of the donkeys and the zebras, and as they sniff it, while their trotting slows down, folds slowly unfold along their bellies and turn inside out and phalluses appear, slimy and blue and, as they expand, drag along the ground, and then with the crack of a whip a throaty "Hoyraa" sounds from all sides, the waltz breaks off, and now the staves of the black figures thud in a driving rhythm, and then the llama raises its head and joins in the shout: Hoyraa, it yells, hoyraa, hoyraa, shrill, rutting, and the donkeys hesitate, the zebras rear up, the donkeys stop, the camels, with the llama's head above their humps, surge wildly forward, a wave of roaring flesh suddenly fills the sky, and then the Cuman, picking leaves off the wreath and scattering them into the gasping jaws of the stallions, leads the okapi to the head of the procession, and I see that the okapi must be a mare, a sexless god or a mare, and at that moment, in one single scream, the wave surges after her, and in the resuming roar of the waltz and hot smell of smoke and musk, surrounded by the herdsmen, the precious trembling flesh disappears into the salami factory of Herz & Pick

"The secret," says Zoltán, and he did not have to say anything. ... The opal-yellow eyes of the zebras. ... The okapi goddess. ... The milk-white smoke. ...

"The secret," says Zoltán, "now you've smelled it, is a special kind of coal, a specially charred special wood of a type of acacia that only grows down here beside the Tisza

We walk for a long time through the streets, not speaking, down along the river, acacia sky, barges with lanterns and beat music, Orion in the night-blue, and suddenly I understand the Mongolian dream. You'll soon find out what's inside a Mongolian, those were his last words, and suddenly I see it, I see it before me, in large letters, what's inside a MONGolian is a GNOMe

October 29

Back late last evening, lay awake for a very long time;
toward morning at last a shallow sleep; a dream of three
princesses, a well-known fairy-tale motif, and in my dream
carried to complete conclusion in surprising variations, all
of a piece and ready for the press, taking place in Cam-
bodia, stridently shameless, shrill, and reflecting frustra-
tion with triumphant and obscene mockery

As I enter the lobby, commotion: the fat bellboy and the
lady at the foreign-exchange desk are chasing some gypsy
children through the revolving door. Even the gentle,
patient lady at Reception is indignant: "Now they're even
coming into the Astoria, it's time to call out the militia!"
I take the opportunity to ask about my radio again, and
the gentle lady is very amazed – the mechanic had had a
look at it, hadn't he

The animal procession to Herz & Pick – was it a dream,
was it reality? Here I know that it was reality, but I have
had some experiences that meant a lot to me and of which
I can no longer be sure of – a walk under a waterfall, or
an embrace on a flat roof under an icy Ukrainian sky, or
the front quarters of a diagonally severed dog on a mile-
stone, or

what *was* reality: the endless walk through operating
rooms, huge rooms divided by screens in which work was
being done on living people; I walked through them as a
child after splintering my elbow joint at the convent school
and having to be operated on; to this day I can still see
through an opened cheek into the inside of a mouth and
standing in front of it a man laughing and holding a pair

of notched, bloody forceps and around him a circle of laughing white figures

and then I was given some sandwiches with plump whole sardines and whole tiny sausages and a glass of tea, and I sat in a deep armchair, and white stretchers were wheeled past, this was also reality

Reality: the air raid on the brain-damaged patients in the school in Jena

Reality: the woman who as she groaned started to pray aloud and gasped out her prayer

Reality is Weinert's voice in the Wehrmacht barracks at Kharkov, and drawings and etchings by Renoir and Cézanne under coal sacks in the cellar of a tiny secondhand book store in the eastern part of Berlin

Reality, too, the entry of Apollyon: the report about the professor being beheaded by a streetcar is true

At breakfast, Gábor with his unbelievable briefcase. I tell him about the gypsy children being driven out of the hotel, and he advises me not to trust appearances and to guard against false romanticism. The kids, their enchanting impertinence, their eyes, their grubby curls, sure, but at the next street corner their fathers or uncles or grandmothers or older brothers turn them upside down and empty their pockets and beat them up when they suspect them of keeping something back. ... If one wants to do the kids a good turn, he said, give them chewing gum, that was the only thing the grownups let them keep

At the next table, the old lady who drinks three large steins of beer every morning, that's reality too

As for the gypsies, according to Gábor they move in mysterious swarms through the country, like clouds of birds through the air which sometimes scatter apart only to flock together again abruptly; in this way they might assemble unexpectedly beside a river, in a valley, outside a town, a cloud of carts, begging and violins, and since last week they had been arriving from the *puszta* and were surrounding Budapest in growing throngs

On my way to see Ferenc, that sudden deadening feeling on the banks of the Danube: on each of my visits I deliberately took a walk along the Belgrade Quay here and looked up at a window, trying to summon enough courage to go to the nearest phone and inquire whether a visit would be convenient, and now it is forever too late

"Forever" – you won't grasp that until later

What was it that so fascinated me on first reading Lukács? Surely, strange as it sounds, least of all what was "Lukács" in what I was reading, least of all what was specific, most of all (perhaps exclusively) what was general! It was my first experience of the Other in intellectual terms, my first encounter with Marxism, with dialectics, with materialism – how could I possibly have discovered the individual element in the writing! That someone (or rather: that a method) should see relationships, lines, processes, inherent laws, where we were accustomed only to barren dates, dates in the framework of dates and intertwined with the names of inspiring beloved ones, an intertwining that was then supposed to have given rise to a literary work, a

Marienbad Elegy or a *West-East Divan* or a *Faust* or some such thing: that these things should be interrelated, that there should be intellectual relationships, relationships between the intellectual and the historical, for instance the relationship between a literary decline and a lost revolution or that between an Old Believer patriarch and revolutionary Russian peasants – all this was quite simply a revelation, and what took my breath away was the emergence of my own fate as I suddenly grasped from books: *Tua res agitur*

In war literature, for example, the irresistible fascination of the crudest depictions of battles and atrocities: that was *my* experience, how could it possibly turn up in literary history

Or Nietzsche and barbarism; or Rilke and barbarism; or philistines and barbarism, it was my very own thing, and even Tolstoy was suddenly my very own thing, and this upheaval was suddenly invaded by the reports about Nuremberg and Auschwitz

As if it were in *hora mortis*: I knew nothing of Auschwitz, knew nothing about Auschwitz. ... This "What did I know?" was something I have always wanted to write; I always saw it as a story, but a single page would probably suffice

Of course at that time I was reading as a Fascist, how else? ... The actual core in Lukács, his digression on democracy and the fateful role of its absence in German history, was something I completely failed to understand – indeed, I failed even to notice it

And the poems that I scribbled every evening on a wooden shingle before attending antifascist school and had to scratch out again every morning with a piece of broken glass because all I had was one shingle – they were nothing more than the continuation of my evening scribbles as a soldier and yet were not and yet were

And yet were not: Auschwitz was in them

And yet were

And yet were not: S became P

And yet were

Or – and that was already in the antifascist school when I was reading Engels, *Dialectics of Nature* and *Anti-Dühring* and *Feuerbach* – at that time I drew on a quarter of the precious piece of paper that was supposed to last for eight hours of lessons a cross of coordinates marking the north pole with "MA" and the south pole with "ID" and the west pole with "me" and the east pole with "di," and then in the southeast I wrote HEGEL and in the southwest PLATO and in the northwest FEUERBACH BÜCHNER AND MOLESCHOTT, and when our teaching assistant asked me aghast what in Heaven's name I was thinking of, wasting all that paper, I proudly replied that I was designing a diagram of philosophy which would take care of every philosophical school and doctrine: above materialism, below idealism, on the left metaphysics, on the right dialectics, and the assistant nodded enthusiastically, and then we both wondered where we should put Kant's agnosticism, described by Lenin as "bashful materialism"; we ended up putting it at top right in north-north-

northeast, and I began to outline a SCHEME OF DIA-
LECTICS

With Zoltán and Jutta to the movies: *Cold Days*. This is
a film one will never forget. ... The frozen Danube, the
dull, faintly booming explosions. ... Those eyes. ... And
then the eternally circling question: Whoever counted the
dead, how could they ever know how many there were,
who could possibly have counted the dead

Terrible variation of a nursery song, "Can you count the
stars above you

My generation has arrived at Socialism via Auschwitz. All
reflection on our change must begin at the gas chamber,
and nowhere else

And when did our change come to an end

October 30

Got up early; my daily Hungarian lesson. I could weep, I forget the words in minutes, or rather: I don't absorb them in the first place. And yet Jutta learned Hungarian in four months and speaks it so well that a Hungarian takes her for a native. She speaks it best, incidentally – so I am told – when she is excited, and simply superbly when she is incensed and swears

The subjective-objective conjugation: it greatly complicates the grammar, but, by its differentiating between general and specific statements ("I take a road" – "I take this road") it should offer great possibilities for the literary craftsman. It is interesting that in certain cases these types of conjugation relate to each other as language does to meta-language. "I say words": "*Szavakat mondok*"; "I say: 'words'" (i.e., "words" here as an element of meta-language): "*Szavak mondom*

Hungarian has no word for "to have," one has to paraphrase it. May we draw some conclusion from this as to the national character: the proverbial hospitality? Perhaps

I really have to laugh: here I am pursuing the psychology of peoples – and all I know is a few people, all of one level, namely my own! I know no more about the Hungarian worker than I do about the Hungarian peasant, how dare I be so presumptuous

Spent all day working; gave *Nagyon fáj* its first polish; plus one of József's love poems in free verse and a few of György's aggressive/scurrilous lyric Onta; I find the following especially good:

The Meadow

The shepherd is crawling on all fours around the flock, and
from time to time barks wearily. The sheepdog
sits in the cool shade, a pipe between its teeth.
The moonlight shines red-hot and scorches the
grass.

The sheep, like sluggish gray-white soapsuds on the move,
flow apart in stupid dignity and spill over the
edge of the pasture.

The shepherd's tongue is lolling out. Parched panting.
Then he trots off again on all fours, mulling over
vital recommendations for which – as he well
knows – there is no time now.

József Attila: *You Are So Foolish*

You are so foolish.
You race
like the morning wind.
A car may hit you,
and here I've scrubbed my little table, and now
the soft light of my bread shines more purely.
Why not come back? If you like
I'll buy a blanket for my iron bedstead.
A simple gray blanket
to match
my poverty, and the Lord Himself
will like it very much, and the Lord
loves me too.
He never comes with dazzling radiance,
not wanting to ruin
my eyes

which long so much to see you.
They will look at you very gently,
I will kiss you carefully,
not tear your coat off you,
and I will tell you the many funny things
I have thought up since then
to amuse you.
You will blush,
you will lower your eyes and we will laugh aloud
so that the close-mouthed, grim-faced workers in our
neighorhood can hear us,
they too will smile in their tired, broken dreams.

In the afternoon to the movies, through the streets of the
Mándy district: long, narrow, gray, straight streets, intersecting at right angles, of neo-baroque tenements, all six
stories high but with no inner courtyards, not many restaurants, not many bars either; many artisans' shops; tobacco
stores; grocery stores; stationery stores; several hair-
dressers; screeching streetcars; a secondhand book store
with lots of thrillers and popular science

And the movies, the movies. ... The question of whether
the movie is dying out simply does not arise here. The
reason is not merely, and probably not mainly either, that
the television network is not yet as dense as elsewhere: the
films offered are incomparably greater in number and
variety than, say, in our country; most of the films are
shown with the original sound track and subtitles, so they
can't cost very much, and everyone can pick according to
his taste: wide screen, rerun, old hat, award winner, ex-
periment, sobstuff, shorts, thriller, filmed stage play, kitsch
too, dreamland too, and multinational from Japan to Chile
and Greenland to India

Antonioni's *Zabierski Point*: shown long ago in first-run theaters, but still to be caught here. After this film I understood more about the civil-war-like conditions in the U.S. than from all reports and articles put together. ...

Chaste orgiastics

The cheap shamelessness of so many stale love scenes, none of which go beyond the limits of prudery, and as their counterpart the equally cheap climaxing with a naked woman or an obscenity within the framework of the permitted and the conventional

Is the revolutionary virtue of modesty to be found in the What or the How? Only in the How, so it would seem. Yet that which in literature we call a taboo always refers to a What, to a theme, to a subject, to a happening, to "passages." For literature, taboos of that kind would be inadmissible. This would leave taboos in the How – can they exist? And can the How really be separated from the What, is not the What created from the How? However that may be, what is so often forgotten in this connection is that, in the society which produced it, the taboo was not absolutely inviolable; it was part of its very nature to be violated on certain, very important occasions. In this sense I would be in favor of taboos in art: as a demand for exceptional content and form in those places where a subject requires them. A taboo is that which allows no mediocrity: great or not at all. And in those countries where the taboo originated, the unanimous word for its counterconcept is: common

The cost of breaking taboos should be high, but it must be possible to break them

The everyday use of taboo words signifies a speeding up of language inflation, nothing more. The sexual sphere seems to be the only one in which some words for extreme meanings have not yet become threadbare, words for what agitates, enraptures, horrifies, enchants, dismays, shocks, drives you mad, and they should be saved up for these meanings and used only when they cannot be replaced by any others. The mindless, leveling use of such words is evidence of the same attitude toward language as the mindless use of "grand," "colossal," "monstrous," "historic hour" and so on

In a taboo, if it deserves this name, social and personal reticence coincide, but apart from the social taboo there also exists the personal taboo, and that includes everything which is protected by modesty and hence also by reverence: in other words, the private sphere with its core of the intimate sphere and its aura of family and circle of friends. During certain eras, this personal taboo has also included an inclination toward art. Young people are sometimes ashamed to show their poems or even admit to writing them. For them it is a confession, touching upon all that is most intimate. ... Personally I prefer this attitude to the hawking of conveyor-belt poems, although I must admit that most of the reticent poets are terrible duffers and soon give up. But maybe it is precisely this reticence that prevents them from transcending the conventional, the cliché, and discourages them before they have found a voice of their own

The widespread reluctance at being watched while at work

According to a good rule, a poem, a story, a book, that one does not have to write should be left unwritten; but one should also put aside any piece during the writing of which one did not have to fight against feelings of reticence. But perhaps I have no business generalizing from my own experience

"Dirt is matter in the wrong place" – in this sense I am in favor of cleanliness. It is a question of determining one's place, in other words of determining this wrong or right place, and in literature this means: one's function. Goethe's distinction of not making a subject great by means of an image (in the widest sense) but making an image great by means of a subject, also applies, and particularly so, to the sexual or intimate sphere – not from prudishness but precisely in the name of great erotic art

"The loss of shame is the first sign of feeblemindedness" (Freud; freely cribbed). I don't want any feebleminded books

Great shamelessness presupposes the overcoming of great shame, not the covering up of a little shame, that is merely vulgar. Total absence of shame is a natural phenomenon, and in that case the word "shamelessness" loses its meaning

Someone says: I am free to say anything I like, and as a proof he shouts an obscenity about his mother at the audience and challenges you to do likewise. It would not be a sign of freedom to follow suit, and this also applies if you replace the mother by a social authority. But I must reserve the right to utter an analogous phrase under certain compelling, immutable circumstances if by doing so I can achieve something that is absolutely necessary and attainable only by uttering such a phrase

179

In saying that the cost of breaking a taboo should be high, I am thinking solely of criticism, but of the kind that touches upon the roots. In a Socialist society such criticism might once again become a moral institution, but we do not have even the rudiments of either, neither criticism nor publicity

In this context the very interesting remark by Ferenc that the layman generally thinks of Vienna when he hears or refers to Hungary's relationship to German culture, but that is exactly where the layman goes wrong. Intellectual Hungary, he says, and Budapest in particular, has always been on the defensive toward Vienna while sensing an affinity with Berlin, with the critical spirit of that city, its artistic relentlessness, its principle of quality, its setting of standards

What, I wonder, is the relationship between change and taboo? As a young Fascist, was I conscious of taboos, or was I not even aware of the notion? Was Hitler taboo to me? There is no quick answer to this, but I believe that Hitler was not, whereas the concentration camps were

There were thoughts that one did not want to think, such as that of a possible defeat. Here there actually emerged something like a taboo in the totemistic sense, and it was not fear of the scaffold that made one recoil from the subject. ... Jokes could also cost you your life, yet you kept on telling them. ... It was something else: there was a kind of tacit agreement not to touch on such questions, and that is precisely what a taboo is, an agreement to let sleeping dogs lie, a sort of intimate sphere of society

On the morning of May 4, 1945, when I was drinking my coffee in my parents' house, without saying a word, and then got up, without saying a word, slung my pack on my back and limped out: toward the final victory

Similar taboo-like situations in the monastery school too; I recall how I agonized over the problem of the criminal Popes and that of the Inquisition and witch-burnings, and how I never dared express any of this, and was afraid that merely by my thoughts I had committed a sin against the Holy Ghost, that sin which is never forgiven. ... Until at the start of my second year at school my father confessor called me out of the classroom one day and with a troubled expression asked me why I did not trust him and reveal my doubts to him: during vacation I had, after all, been out in the world, and surely I, the monastery-school boy, the pious, devout child, a constant vexation to the wicked, must have been needled by such questions as that about the vice-ridden Popes or the Inquisition or the witch-burning, and he could not believe that these barbs were not painful, and I nodded shamefacedly and said: "Yes, Father, that's how it was," and Father Kornelius Barycs went for a walk with me in the park and talked about the vice-ridden Popes and talked about atrocities that made me shudder, and we walked slowly beneath the morning stars of the chestnut trees, and my father confessor said: "And you see, my boy, so great is the power of our Holy Church that even a man like Alexander the Sixth, when he spoke *ex cathedra*, pronounced the unbending, true and eternal Word of God, so great, my boy, so holy, so wonderful and powerful and so confirmed in Grace is our Mother, *ecclesia nostra*, and now go and kneel down and worship!" and I rushed into the chapel, and from the gold and rubies an angel descended, and I saw Alexander's sad face in the flames, it was merely sad, surprised and sad, and I folded my hands and prayed for him

Taboo and change: anyone in a totem society who broke a taboo became taboo himself; protoform of a change that lives on in the transformation of animals in fairy tales

A taboo never applied to an enemy, it always appeared (and appears) within one's own life-sphere. Moreover, it was always associated with the clan, and its appearance probably had something to do with the division of labor. Might one say that it is a manifestation of the contradiction between man the creature of nature and man the creature of society

Every taboo in literature is raised by the writer himself, and it only becomes taboo by my acceptance of it, and it is only then that it becomes a literary problem

Is there a connection between loathing and taboo? Certainly, but every kind of loathing? I hesitate

Walking home in the scent of chestnuts

Discovery on Chain Bridge: it's possible to walk around the triumphal arches

Zabierski Point – what a role the landscape plays! True, not everyone has a desert with chalky dust and canyons, but even in Mark Brandenburg or in Mecklenburg there are other things than the eternal lake with the eternal reeds with the eternal topless girl

This topless-audacity always reminds me of Roda Roda's nice little story: "I'd like to see anyone follow my example – dance all through the third night of the regimental ball like my daughter Ottilie. ..."

As a young man I read somewhere, possibly something by Romano Guardini, that botanical processes such as a bud opening or a blossom closing, when filmed in accelerated motion appear shameless since they show movements which the Creator had intended to be concealed by Nature's slow process. I was fascinated by this observation and found it confirmed in a documentary I saw in a small military hospital in Silesia. I watched it as I sat beside a nurse with whom I was in love, Countess S., and I made up my mind to start a conversation with her about Guardini, but we never got around to it, the Red Army began its January offensive, the hospital was hastily evacuated, and I never saw her again. ... That was also the time when my left foot was to be amputated; I had agreed to the operation and it had already been scheduled, but then, as I said, the Red Army broke through the Vistula front and we fled – a whole lot of movie stories

This accelerated-motion effect only shows up in film, in literature it has the opposite effect

A four-dimensional historical atlas, that would be a thrill

There is something that is slowly but irresistibly growing more and more pressing (stronger, more challenging, louder, sharper, shriller, more and more imperative): the Hamlet sequence, a force which, like no other, can bring me to my knees, and which, whenever I sense it anywhere, I invariably face up to

The most fascinating effect of literature I have ever run across: that passage in Kellermann's *Tunnel* when the engineer (I have forgotten his name, I have forgotten everything except this particular passage and the one about the elephant ride along Broadway, and for the sake of this memory I shall never read the novel again), when that engineer enters the burning tunnel breasting the tide of those escaping from it. ... If it is possible to express ethics in movement, then this is it

A sudden inspiration for a literary dice game, and for an instant the serious desire to jump into the Danube

Móricz – I knew some of his stories; now I am reading a volume of short stories almost without stopping as far as the middle and am overwhelmed

The concept of tragedy expands – with us, Ferdinand loves Luise and cannot have her; there a poor devil who is allowed for the first time after forty years of starvation to eat his fill at his employers' wedding feast and is already full after the soup and in desperation works his way through twelve courses until he eats himself to death

A fairy tale – no, more, decidedly more: a myth

In "The Cloudgazers" a striking parallel to Thomas Mann's "The Path to the Cemetery": something new, crude, brutal, extraordinarily self-assured appears on the scene and immediately proves to be all-determining

I don't know why, but in reading one sentence of this story I suddenly recall the hyena keeper at the Leipzig Zoo, who shook his fist at a female animal which had devoured two of its newborn whelps during the night and swore at it, believing in all seriousness that it was now slinking away in shame, but he would never forgive such a wickedness

I keep wondering: why didn't I laugh during that movie? This question, although I have so far not been able to answer it, is valid, and so is the question: How were you affected by this discovery of forced labor being imposed on the dying? But there is absolutely no sense in the very natural question: So why didn't you break with the Nazis, why didn't you defect, why didn't you resist, and so on? Yet this is the very question that is always being asked, especially by young people. They have a right to this question, of course, only that they demand from each single impact the immediate and direct effect of the sum of the impacts which finally brings about the break. To be sure, the last drop that causes the glass to overflow is also just a drop like the preceding ones, but it happens to be the last one, and many others had to precede it, and each one was necessary, and often drops fell into the glass that were bigger than that last one, and when they fell their sole effect was one of preparation, of indispensable preparation for that one last drop

"Uncompleted change" – is there such a thing

S has not become P, that is a tragedy

It is the old story of Sleeping Beauty: hundreds of knights had to perish miserably in the thicket, and it was for only one of them, the last, that the gate opened, and he won the princess, and there was no injustice in that

There is no such thing as historical automatism, the "premature ones" are necessary, without them there is no "later," without them stagnation, duration without history, "Chinese" or "Arabic" eras

Even the tardy ones at one time had a chance of becoming the premature ones, they merely failed to avail themselves of it

Ants, when they are on the move and come to a ditch: enough of them fall in to fill the ditch, and the migration continues. True, not everyone who falls into a ditch is a forerunner. ... And anyway, whose forerunner would such an ant be? This idea doesn't fit in here at all

"Forerunner" and "foregoer": strangely enough, these two words appear to have no connection with the distinction between "to run" and "to go

Do you become aware of each of these impacts, these "drops," or did you ever become aware of each one of them? This is worth thinking about

An old saying: In every human being a poet has died. ... But: How many poets *had* to die in him to enable him to become the particular human being he is

Is a forerunner someone who breaks a taboo or calls it into question or merely happens to discover that a taboo exists

Are there unknown taboos? Undiscovered taboos? Tabooed taboos? Is there a taboo behind every axiom? Were there ever tabooless societies? Is a taboo always linked to religion? Might the Communist society be a tabooless society? So many questions

Such questions can only occur to one in Budapest

Has a forerunner brought about a change, or does he bring changes in his wake? Does he move away from society, or does he move the coming society toward him

To set one's own person as a yardstick

To set oneself a taboo in order to have to break it

To try to master seemingly insuperable difficulties by adding one more to them – it actually helps

The What is an immense, good-natured fatted calf, the How a rat

The What has three dimensions, the How is the fourth

How: What = Nevertheless: The Less

What is contained in "nevertheless" is obvious: "never the less!" But do we see the "how ever" in "however"? "Nevertheless" is avant-garde, "however" is rearguard

Nonetheless

October 31

Up early; no dream; a crystal-clear day, crystal-blue sky, and off by bus to Dömös to István's cabin

At the bus terminal there are twenty-six buses ready to go in every possible direction, although all you need is one going to Dömös. Such overabundance always amazes you, and you're forever making the great discovery: Others travel too, and to other places too

István's cabin turns out to be a roomy old farmhouse with a covered walkway, trapdoor and cellar, attic, workshop, huge cooking range, very low ceilings; an outdoor dining table, a shed full of firewood, an overgrown garden going down to the brook, and in the garden a garden of Baltic Sea pebbles

The brook – it doesn't look as if it could wash away Dömös, and yet it has gardens, buildings, even people on its conscience

In the garden a piece of quartz like a set of tiger's teeth

Hungarian courtesy: When I tell István about the child of my daughter (whom he knows), he says: "Well, well, that would almost make you a grandpa

At the fence next door a young fellow wearing studded trousers with brown fur patches on knees and seat, and an old peasant, in black, holding a long willow branch

Two black-and-white cats, one of them almost geometrically black and white in trapezes running spirally to its

neck; the other pure white with a black nose and
black muzzle, both black spots forming perfect black cir-
cles

In the covered walkway outside the kitchen, two dozen
bottle gourds hanging from strings: elongated shapes,
green, juice-laden, with very long, generously curved necks
that abruptly merge into fat bellies with oddly twisted
skins. The gourds are bursting with juice and strength and
greenness, only one of them seems incurably ill: in two
places, each as big as a hand, the skin is discolored, going
from purple to gray, two eczema-like gangrenous patches,
but they are not scabby or crusty, i.e., not a layer imposed
over something healthy underneath but rather the skin
rotting away with the flesh itself. This gourd is much
lighter, too, a victim of putrefaction, it seems to be devouring itself; and when I ask István why he doesn't throw it
out and whether he wasn't afraid that the sick gourd would
infect the healthy ones, he laughs aloud, his chin bouncing,
and tells me that it is just beginning to look nice, they
would all change like that, those green fellows, those
stupid, fat, overweight characters, they would evaporate
their useless water and become light, feather-light and
long-lasting, lasting for many years, and beautiful, in an
interplay of colors, each one an individual and of an
astonishing intelligence in coloring the shape

Beside the gourds a blackjack, a lead ball on a brass chain,
and István explains that his son András had made it for
himself when they moved here and the village youths had
threatened to lynch him if he dared touch one of the girls,
even if she was the ugliest; and István adds that András
had never used the thing but had needed it

I am still looking at the bottle gourds; István chooses one as a gift for me, and now I notice pear-shaped spots on its belly shimmering purplish brown

I am reminded of Hoffmann's privy councilors

Walk through the village: the houses nearly all of one type – breast-high walls around the spacious yard; the house set far back, ground and upper floor, stone foundation; gables facing the street, many of them containing circular, embrasure-like windows, the other windows small casements; covered walkway; the façades in bright colors: yellow, white and pale yellow, ornamented with burgundy red and blue, or white and green

Outside almost every house a bench; two stone supports, a red wooden seat, a red wooden back, and on most of the backs in white lettering: LOTTO TOTTO

Everywhere a wonderful smell of smoke: the scented hallmark of the kingdom of Man under Heaven

Along the street at the outer edge of a zone between street and sidewalk, stocky little acacia trees, their tops at head-level; between the little trees and the sidewalk, roses; between the sidewalk and the farmyards, flowerbeds bordered by a strip of gravel. The acacias here still in full leaf, but among them a few trees standing completely bare, with knobbly, grotesquely twisted branches, bent this way and that, meaningless and beautiful

The sky crystal-clear, crystal-blue, the mountains etched in profile against the sky

Hyper-precision of contour can alienate the object to the point of being unrecognizable: reduction to one dimension

Down to the Danube: on this side the village, sloping up-hill from the river, embedded in high hills; the Danube a U, and the loop of its opposite banks filled with massive heights

The slopes across the river: very steep, slate, shrubs, no forest, a few vertical rock walls and in them caves like tunnel entrances – does a railway run through there? Inconceivable, but what else could it be

The brook rushes downhill. "Such a thin little thread, it's impossible to believe it could flow into the Danube, but the Danube does not scorn it. ..." You mull over a sentence like that, and of course you immediately discover a partiality for the river inherent in such words: The flowing of the brook into the big river is shown to be a favor on the part of the powerful one. So: "The brook is such a thin little thread that it's impossible to believe it could flow into the Danube, yet it even defies a separating wall of mud!"

Hah! Now the brook is being wooed. So we notice: on either side of the brook shoulder-high weeds, and in the rivulet all the junk from the village: blue pots, automobile tires, gasoline containers, oilcans, empty kegs, plastic bags, rusty tubes, pop bottles, cans, Nivea tins, orange and sky-blue plastic, a battered suitcase, a disemboweled radio, broken china, sardine cans, a tape-recorder spool. In Berlin I once saw a documentary on burial customs in the Hungarian plains, medieval ceremonies, female litanies, white rites, the widow walking slowly around the bier while chanting traditional formulas of grief; the impression down here provides the necessary contrast

Poplars like willows: long shoots, green and pale gray, rising from stumps

Acacia thorns as large as hobnails

Two pop bottles up to their bellies in the water; they are moralizing together

What's this: along the path lie piles of foot-long fruit pods, flat, brownish blue, looking like blades, two inches wide, very flat, filled with loose, rattling seeds and curved like Turkish swords

Under a very tall, very slender acacia, hundreds of such pods, apparently quite ignored by the children: whatever can they be? The closest comparison would be with carob beans, but completely flat, a lot longer and wider, more regular in shape, and no black in their color

On the opposite bank – what I called "shrubs" turn out to be trees, a deciduous forest, and tall trees, I can now compare them with the telegraph poles, and the trees, although, well beyond them, are considerably taller

On this side: gray grass, containing large burned patches and gray debris. (If you emphasize the first syllable of debris, it sounds quite Hungarian; I wonder whether it means anything? Think up an object to go with this designation, or a person, and invent his biography: Leo Débris, advertising expert from Győr, born 1907

Change of meaning through shift in stress, e.g., "invalid" and "invalid" lots of fun, and nice collector's items too

The blue Danube – here it *is* blue, for the sky is blue and it mirrors the sky. You can change its color by taking two steps forward or back and letting it mirror alternately the gray heights and the blue sky. That's crazy. ... ("*in*valid" and "in*val*id," that's crazy too!) In point of fact it is obvious, a truism, but you have to find that out

Can I say: the Danube changes? But is that leap from gray to blue and vice versa *not* a change

Far away on the horizon, beyond the river, where the river meets the sky, a paler wisp – what is it? Mist rising from the water; mist sinking from the sky? Danube and sky are a delicate gray-blue, they would be indistinguishable were they not separated by the minuteness of that whiter wisp. But what is that wisp? Is it a row of hills, a river bank, is it a wisp or is it transition itself, the physical manifestation of an idea

This In-between between Danube and sky is indescribable, like one of those translations into the void which Mallarmé tried to put into words. ... Could language express it, just this, this transition, but precisely *it*? Perhaps; a labor of days, and what would be gained? Much: an insight into what language can do

No: an insight into what you can do, language can do everything

no, don't just write down something, think about it: can language really do everything? Negative examples come pouring in: smells, tastes, nuances of light and shade, concrete atmospheres that are indescribable, such as: the smell of overripe Limburger cheese. But language can express it

precisely: "the smell of overripe Limburger cheese," that is
a perfectly accurate statement, unequivocal, an exact piece
of information, entirely adequate for practical purposes;
you might, for example, order that kind of a perfume or
deodorant with no possibility of confusion. But then one is
unwilling to accept that: it is, one says, a tautology. Not
at all, it is an exact utterance. You have been imagining
some kind of metaphor, but then that's up to you; go on
looking, and if *you* are capable you'll find it. Language has
done its part, and we'll get along nicely without your metaphors

From one particular vantage point, but from that one only,
the Danube seems to be edged with a threadlike white
border which, however, has nothing at all in common with
that wisp (the wisp lies above it

Not only must the sky be blue and one's position carefully
chosen for the Danube to appear blue: it must also be completely motionless. Far away on the other shore a little
boat, and the ripples caused by its oars would be imper-
ceptible, but they would be enough to extinguish the blue

Now instead of "blue" one might say: "reflecting the un-
clouded daytime sky from an unruffled surface into the eye
of the observer." True enough, but this would only apply
to the blue of an object with reflecting qualities and not to
the blue of a harebell. Yet one doesn't say: "The mirror is
blue" when it reflects the sky! But one insists on saying it
of the Danube! So that as yet nonexistent adjective would
indeed be useful! It would release the Danube from a reproach; however, it would also deprive generations of
tourists of a witticism, husbands of a joke, patresfamilias
of a morsel of authority

A gull flaps by; it looks abnormally large, one could swear it was another breed

Distinguishing between a quality that is innate and one that is simulated by mere reflection, and the pinpointing of this distinction by various words: this might be worthwhile, particularly in the field of aesthetics; let's say, the difference between literature of a socialist content and a literature that merely reflects socialism or even merely reflects the reflection of socialist ideas

Goethe's distinction between an object that achieves greatness by means of an image, and an image that achieves greatness by means of an object, as a distinction between mythology and mythologem. This passage helped me over a crisis in my *Prometheus*, as did one of Herder's essays

At first I wanted to narrate the Prometheus material as a fairy tale, and in fact I do start out in quite a fairy-tale mood. But it became impossible to cope with this material in terms of a fairy tale: the moral attitude of Cronus had to be distinguished from that of Zeus, and both from that of Prometheus, in principle rather than only by degree. That, however, put the story beyond the limits of the fairy tale; Prometheus' progress from the Titans via the gods to men could no longer be told in terms of a fairy tale. I was forced to take the step to the myth

Why has nature poetry almost died out? Granted, describing nature at second or third hand, perpetuating traditional images that have long since ceased to correspond to reality is tiresome, annoying, but then that applies to any subject matter. The city landscape: now that would be worth pursuing, but not for us any more, for we have no real cities, we only have large small-towns (and I mean this in an entirely positive sense). Another possibility would be the discovery of the growing shabbiness of the landscape, its decay, its devastation, its transformation into garbage dumps (in the broadest sense); there are already signs of this, in Nezval and Halas, for instance, and also some elements in Maurer. And now comes the regeneration of the landscape – might that be a theme? One's first impulse is to say no – obviously one's mind goes immediately to that perpetuating of romantic landscape images. But must landscape poetry be like that? Might not a new generation produce something new

"All paths are correct, as long as you keep going." That was said by Barlach, and it keeps recurring to me, and I keep doubting it, as I do now

Very well, let's take this path then, parallel to the shore, some fifty yards from it, some three feet wide, made of fine, tamped-down, pale-yellow gravel that looks like cement but crumbles easily, and it runs parallel to the village street, ending in the street that forms the boundary of the village up the slope: keep going

This example was meant as a playful attempt at reducing Barlach's words *ad absurdum*, but in a truly absurd way Barlach turns out to be right: walking a few hundred yards farther along this very path you discover that that wispy line between river and sky that you were unable to describe is quite clearly a range of hills, clearly articulated, fairly high and massive, clearly rising above the river, clearly under the blue sky, and it is totally inconceivable that this could ever have been a wisp

The cement path has come to an end; leading up to the village street, a kind of ridge, between gardens of willow trees, with black water trickling down both flanks: keep going

Apple orchards; squashed, rotting apples on the ground, squashed tomatoes among them, and swarms of small insects circling above them in the shape of blunt, sharply outlined cones

Sea-green cabbage gone to seed, an amiable, corpulent rose

A large duck, frightened by a cat

Smell of smoke and sourish ordure

Sudden memory of having dreamed last night after all, and of buying an orchid in my dream, and then, as if an invisible curtain were jerked aside, the memory that, earlier in the dream, I had walked through a forest, a forest with a clear green sheet of water under which lay the interlacing red paths. ... Silence; the knee-deep water lay motionless, and I was afraid to enter it; I stood in a trance at its edge, looking in rapture at the indescribable deep-green purity and, below it, the ornament of the paths as they ran together and apart; not a sound was to be heard, not a tremor, not a movement; I stood and looked and reached mechanically for the notebook in my pocket, to register this scene, but put it back again immediately, thinking: No, don't write! Don't turn this magic into paper

It was the same determination with which I tore up and threw into the fire the diary I had already begun about my grandchild: to have a piece of life that does not dissolve into ink, with no ulterior motive of literary usefulness

Or that mean, furtive pleasure of thinking up a story or a poem and finishing it in your head and then letting it drop back into formlessness and watch it go under. This, by the way, would be the only attitude to justify the term "free lance

Now once again I see the colors in this dream: that green, that red. ... Is it possible that there are colors in a dream which the waking eye cannot see? I don't mean hitherto unperceived shades of colors of the rainbow, but colors which the rainbow does not contain, colors not produced by combinations of yellow, red and blue? I imagine so; I once dreamed about a sea voyage where I saw waves of indescribable incomparable colors; I can no longer evoke them, I only know that they were different, in an illusory approach: a black-purple that was at the same time gold

Jet streams in the sky, they too are part of the landscape

Just before I reach the village street, a little old woman carrying an enormous bunch of pale-mauve asters in both arms, as if come to welcome the Prodigal Son: me

Sunday before All Souls' Day. ... swarms of children with enormous bunches of flowers, with baskets full of flowers, they are very serious, very dignified, not at all mischievous, and the men in black coats and black suits, their silvery hair looking as if acquired especially for this day

To go through all the provinces of Hungary, no, all the provinces of Europe, and pick a bunch of flowers for the dead Cumans and a little bunch of snowdrops and cowslips for Princess Margit, she is such a nice saint. ... There is a lovely poem about her by Ady: many courted her, but she waited for that other one, and when the other did not come she declined and died in a convent

The story of Sleeping Beauty in reverse

If I were a Catholic, I would pray to Saint Margit

All Souls' Night, and up the Danube float the drowned of all rivers and all seas, floating up to Margit Island, salt-bearded, with white, salt-eyed faces and pickled eyes, and they climb on land and bed down under the elms and howl and howl, Icarus and Odysseus' crew and Hero and the Unknown Woman and the drowned Negroes of the slave ships and Margit, who drowned in the muddy water, and the women emerge from the old walls and wash and murmur and wash: Ho, Shem and Shaun, all sons of Livia's daughters, dark falcons hear us! Ho, aom! poum! pyoum!, and the sea wind whistles and the dead howl as they plunge into the water and swim out and perish, All Souls' Night

So many flowers, and you're always thankful you don't know their names. ... Not so with trees, those you have to know; the difference has something to do with that between prose and poetry

Past a herd of white geese stalks a totally black cat coming directly from Egypt. ... Very large, pointed, cone-shaped ears, its rump on high legs, almost like a dog or a small hyena, but the tail like that of a wildcat's: blunt, thick, kinked

Dwarf acacias: an ostrich that has lost its feathers, just a bunch left on its rump

Black sheepdogs, with thick coats, coats like whiplashes, only the tongue revealing which end is the front, the fur seems matted with grease and falls in dense, pencil-thick, foot-long tassels indiscriminately over eyes, flanks, thighs and rumps, you can't see their eyes but they can see you

A side street where all the houses are red, their walls studded with blue, green and purple pottery shards

I am reminded of the winegrower in Szigliget, four years ago: he was building a new house, the whole village was building new houses, they simply moved a bit up the slope, leaving the old village where it was, and built afresh, it looked like a picture by Brueghel. I asked him about police regulations governing building and he didn't understand. I tried to explain, but he said, shaking his head: "What's the police got to do with it? The police aren't going to live there, it's *my* head it'll collapse on if I don't build right

For lunch a soup with whole fist-size onions, the soup cooked around them; and gypsy roast, and cauliflower and carrots baked together in a soufflé: cauliflower and carrots: I regard the alliteration as being in my honor

Could one make up menus in this way? An ABC book of menus, why not? For instance (in honor of Dömös) D: Date soup; Danube pike; saddle of Deer with Dumplings and Dill pickles; Dobosh cake; Dutch cheese; Drambuie

Bright flash

As we eat, little Gábor is playing with a rag doll and a rag dog; the dog is a three-legged horse that can fly; the doll is called Lukács, which means Luke. The horse wants to ride to the cemetery, and Lukács is blindfolded so he won't be scared by the ghosts, but he is scared anyway, and so he is tied up and given a spanking. "Szegény Lukács; poor Luke," I say, and everybody is mystified, and finally the mystery is cleared up, the doll is called Gábor like Gábor; in Dömös, all Gábor's dolls are called Gábor, and Gábor (the doll) is *lyukas*, meaning holey, it has holes in its head; genesis of a myth

István clears up many of my questions – the strange, blade-like pods, for instance, are wild carob beans that grow only in a very few places in Hungary

And the hill on the other side with the caves, that's Saint Michael's Hill, it consists of tuff, hence the caves, and that's why it was once inhabited by monks of a Greek Orthodox order that had made a vow to live only in caves, and its members settled wherever they found tuff, as they did here. Every village child, says István, has spent a night there, it is very warm in there, and it is considered a test of courage which no boy may shirk; and then, says István, a draft dodger once lived in there, he had claimed to be a successor of the monks and announced his intention of founding a new sect; a handsome youth, and three times a day some girl or woman from the village, always a different one, had brought him the necessities of life, food, drink and themselves, but after three weeks he fled and voluntarily gave himself up

István asks Endre to drive me to Esztergom; he had planned to do so himself but his car had broken down. Night falls quickly. It strikes me that István often calls out: "*Vigyázz balra!*" – "*Vigyázz jobbra!*"; and since it also strikes me that such cries, "Watch out on the left!" – "Watch out on the right!", are always accompanied by the appearance of some obstacle, a bicycle approaching without a light, or a bus, a rock, the Danube, or what have you, I come to the conclusion that Endre must be night-blind, and so in fact he is

He can see practically nothing at night, can't see his hand in front of his face. István steers him from the back seat, and that's how we drive to Esztergom and back to Dömös, and as we get out there I see that Endre is dripping with sweat, and I see it with satisfaction, although still weak at the knees, and Endre wipes the sweat from his forehead and mutters uneasily: "Maybe I shouldn't have driven – my brakes aren't working, you know

Full moon over the golden-yellow round tower of the basilica of Esztergom, and the blown-up bridge over the Danube still lying in the water, and along both banks the melancholy lights

The words "downy evening

In the basilica, a litany for the dead. I understand nothing yet, since I understand the form, I understand everything: I can fill the form, hence I can participate

In the cathedral, bustling father confessors. Could the father confessor understand the penitent if he didn't speak the penitent's language and the penitent didn't speak his? There would be ways of getting around it: he could, for example, number off one commandment after another on his fingers: first, second, third, and a shake of the head would indicate freedom from sin, a nod a confession of sin, and the degree of sinning could be indicated with both hands, like a fisherman

Another bright flash, and this time alarming

Back to Budapest by bus; another chapter of Madách, the crusader scene. Resolution for Berlin: compare with *The Count of Ratzeburg*. Anyway after this trip: another go at Barlach's dramatic works

Madách's dream of mankind passing through the crucial junctures of history from paradise up to the final state of energy-exhausted Earth ought really to be an epic of change (Adam Adam; Adam Pharaoh; Adam Alcibiades; Adam Catullus; Adam Lion-Heart; Adam Kepler; Adam Danton, and so on), but it is an epic of identity

Literature of arrival: in Madách each scene is really an arrival, but the others have always arrived there earlier. And who are the others? Not Adam, of course, since he is the one who is arriving, nor Lucifer, but Eve is always among them

For Madách it is a problem that men kill each other for the sake of an "i":

> "Do you favor
> homoousian or homoiousian?"

But the "i" is merely the symbol of that for which men kill each other. That in this case it is no more than a single letter is amazing; but the amazing part is merely the concentration of the form into a symbol, not the issue itself.

When there are a few more letters it looks quite common-place: (ant)i-fascism – fascism, for instance

"But how can you equate the two! In fascism – antifascism we're not concerned with the four letters a, n, t, i; we're concerned with the crucial struggle between two worlds!" "Were they really concerned with the 'i' at that time?" "But of course – men really and truly fought over that 'i.' The strugghe really was about whether one said 'homoousian' or 'homoiousian!'" "And the life-and-death struggle really and truly was about people saying: 'That's where we must put (against the wall; as head of state; in jail; in the government): a fascist; an antifascist

Strange words: "They must be arrayed in ignominy and shame, those who glorify themselves against me!"

Barlach's life is a life of change *par excellence*. He experienced his Damascus in Güstrow, in a very restricted circle, in everyday life, in the stationer's displays, at officers' casino parties, in the kindergarten, in newspaper headlines, in the waiting room, at the potato dealer's, at the fish market. The beginning was marked by his diary in honor of the Great, the Holy War; the end by: "Therefore let war be cursed. ..."

Thomas Mann: "For the typical is the mythical. ..."

Why don't I write: "He experienced his Auschwitz in Güstrow"? Two answers spring immediately to mind: Auschwitz is much too large for that, says the one; Auschwitz came much later, the other. Both seem most convincing, yet neither is quite satisfying, particularly the first. How many *have* experienced Auschwitz, experienced it physically, and have not changed

But then: *could* they still change after that

So what would be a counter-example, of life of non-change *par excellence*? Napoleon, perhaps; and suddenly a great many names occur to you, and names of such heterogeneous lives that you hesitate to bring them together in one sentence

Change seems to relate to the petty-bourgeois class, to petty-bourgeois intellectuals. Does a worker change? One does not, after all, say he has changed when he becomes a minister of the government or a managing director of a people's industrial complex, what one says is: "He has risen," or: "He has developed"; "He has made use of his possibilities"; "He has shown his potential"; more simply: "He has become a minister of the government," and so on. Nor does one say of a property-owner that he has changed when he loses his property and is proletarianized. But what might subsequently happen to him, to his awareness – that would be called a change. Yet that would be much more of an attempt to harmonize, to get in step, with a change that has already taken place. But might that not be the very essence of a change

Can one define change as a transition to a different value-system (different values or a different order of the old values), as a process which marks the end of the old value-system and with a purification (self-criticism, confession, atonement, penance, retribution, ritual and so forth) begins the new one? That would explain many strange phenomena in camp

Could one say: change is that process within the individual that has become historically necessary for society? In that case the hallmark of a change would be the turning from the reactionary toward the progressive

Fascism scorns the idea of change, finding it redolent of vacillation, non-fanaticism, halfheartedness, impurity (Goebbels: "The Führer has never changed, he has always remained himself!"

Change is an irreversible process; irreversibility is part of its very nature

So a person who has changed would be a person who can no longer go back, only forward; and if he could go back, whatever has happened to him (or whatever he has achieved would not be a change

Jean Paul: "Evening transforms dew to frost, the morning frost to dew."

But why am I playing around with concepts? My life *has* been a change

"Your material is your life, that's what you should examine, that's what you know best!"

A splendid maxim. But: "Your material is your life," that's ambiguous

"Your life is your material" – here the second meaning is almost unrecognizable, arising merely from the memory of the first formulation

"Your life is what you know best" – that's also ambiguous, depending on emphasis. If you say: "Your life is what *you* know best," that's wrong. If I were to assemble all the people who have memories of me, these memories would exceed my knowledge of myself many times. The first years of my life exist only in the memory of others, even my schooldays could be depicted more comprehensively and accurately by my relatives, teachers, classmates and neighbors. How much of what I have suppressed, forgotten, or never become conscious of may exist in the consciousness of others

"*Your* life is what you know best" – is that really true? One might imagine cases – and I know of some – where this does not apply. Finally: "Your *life* is what you know best" – that's not true either. Of all that belongs to you, your life is what you know least; you know your study, your poodle, your vegetable patch much better

Could it be that, from the various aspects of its main emphasis, a sentence is wrong in every case but as a whole, in the sum total of all its aspects, is right? Then part of the concept of a statement would be the concept of the optimum: taking into account every aspect: optimal accuracy

Could one say: optimal lack of ambiguity? And is "lack of ambiguity" an unambiguous concept? And how about "un-unambiguous

What does it mean: "your life"? An unreflected amorphous moment of the Now, and memories. Shouldn't we rather say: "Your life is what you can remember"? But infancy is also part of this "your life," and this we don't remember, whereas Father Kornelius Barycs, whom I do remember, is not my life

Can one say: "Your life is the sum of your memories"?
Certainly not, "your life" is more. Yet the life which is at
our disposal, which is in our possession, which permits us
to act in the present and to think ahead into the future, is
the sum of memories

Is the sum of memories equal to the sum of experiences?
Can one say: "The greater the sum of memories, the greater
the capacity to act"? I suppose so. But is there not also a
forgetting that strengthens, that heals, as a *conditio sine
qua non* of survival? Yes, but first a coming to terms with

To remember, in order to be able to forget. The past that
I can remember is something I have come to terms with,
and through this it has become experience; the other past
has become alienated from me and can overwhelm me
(again and again: the spooky house

"The past that I *can* remember" – this "can" has a triple
meaning: "can" in the sense of "able to"; "can" in the sense
of "being allowed to"; and finally "can" in an unencum-
bered sense, not followed by a "without ... (blushing,
getting sick, hesitating, blenching, etc.

"I forget what I have lived!" – "Forget what I have lived!"
This kind of structural change is amazing; it implies a
strangely deflected wishful thinking

Are there languages that don't have an imperative? And
would one want to live among such people

Are there various types of memories? I believe so. My
memories are mostly needle-sharp and at the same time
often completely rigid images against pale, gray surfaces

as vague as backgrounds in dream-landscapes and sometimes totally bare; images that seem to have a waxworks quality but which sometimes start to move, quite mechanically, as if driven by wheels, functional

Are there cumulative points of such memory-images? And if so, are the most important periods of a life also those with the most memories? This should be carefully examined

"Landscape of memory" – "landscape of dreams" – "landscape of desires" – "landscape of fairy tales" – "landscape of vices and virtues" – that is another little library of wishes

Could memories be crystallized like experiences? Why not? On my desk there might be a row of tiny jars with labels such as "4. 2. 1967 10 h. 32 min. 33 sec.," and so forth, and that would then be my conscious life

If memories can be transformed into printer's ink, why can't they be transformed into salts

The idea of the salts in the little jars is frightening; the idea of holding a book in one's hand and being able to say: "Here I held my conscious life" is satisfying. Why these contrary reactions

The fear of chemistry, the fear of mathematics, the fear of the computer: What is mankind coming to? The fairy tales are falling apart

The earthworm character of some memories: the more one tugs at them the more strenuously they elude one (strenuously? no: stubbornly, steadily, superciliously), and the instant one shifts one's grip they are irretrievably lost (irretrievably for the present, for a certain time, forever). Is this the moment of switching from short-term to long-term memory? Is this "eluding" the evaporating, the dissolving, the withdrawing of a chemical substance, as physiologists maintain? It is quite amazing how often language has pinpointed certain states long before the scientists got to them. "I can't stand the sight of you" is a significant psychological insight, and language, long before science, was aware of that

Would the following be a heuristic method? To take an expression literally and carry it out literally or construct the theory on the basis of taking it literally? That, for instance, was Tyl Eulenspiegel's method and a feature of the method of the good soldier Schweik's method

Uncovering certain memories – they are locked up in a kind of safe to which there is apparently only one key (such as a word, a smell, a sound, a gesture; in reading through the accounts of earlier dreams, it very often happens that for the whole dream to surface in the memory one particular word is required, and suddenly it is all there). The number of these safes and their contents are unknown to us. Can you then say they are part of "your life," of your personality? It seems so: if your life is the sum of all you have lived – and what else should it be? – then these memories are part of your life. But: if you have something within something, and you are unaware of the existence of either – let's say, a legacy of ducats in a Transylvanian castle – can you then say: they belong to me

Sometimes I dream of having committed a murder. ... But perhaps I *have* committed and don't remember it

Salts, alkaloids, certain drugs, can unearth memories. A few of their crystals would be what you are and what you don't know that that's what you are. ... Granted, the key to the safe is not the content of the safe, but: no key, no content

Setting out on the journey to the closed country of memory, to the true Tibet – would one dare? In my dreams I can already look across the frontier. Would I

Does one really become better acquainted with one's own life the more one reflects upon it? ("Acquainted" – odd, as if it were something strange with which one makes acquaintance. So: "more conscious of" – but that is no less odd, as if the essential part of a life were the unconscious!) Doesn't it become increasingly – well, what? vague? mysterious? unmotivated? unmotivatable? impalpable? intelligible? inexplicable? unexplainable? illogical? alogical? or even logical? alien? alienated? alienating? aliening? unreal? incomprehensible? unintelligible? axiomatic? compelling? problematic? problem-free? problem-fraught? straightforward? devious? indeterminable? or all of these, or some of them, or none, or something entirely different

And does this process obscure or illuminate, and might not something become obscurer the more it is illuminated, because the illumination shows up more aspects than one can cope with

Might some of Kafka's parables, the entrance to the law, for instance, be parables of remembering

Do these reflections separate my self from my life? Isn't my pursuit a symptom of schizophrenia? For you do confront yourself, or is the Other who you were a stranger who you never were? Or are you the Other to this day, or are you both today, or have you always been both: the living contradiction

Across the lane, all the shutters are closed; black box; where is the input

November 1

Good God, my reading is set for tomorrow! I turn to a
new story I had brought along just in case, and skimming
through the first page is enough to fill me with such re-
pugnance that I can't go on reading. ... The way the language jogs along instead of flowing smoothly; that ponder-
ous Bohemian provincialism; that wheezing and fussing and
above all that archness I loathe so much and that now
mocks and grins at me from every page

So cutely provincial. Quaint. Adorable. Your immediate
reaction is: "Oooh

Lukács baths, no help there; the mountains, no help there;
secondhand bookstore, no help there

The curse of having no critics to force us to the utmost
limits of our literary potential. ... At the time when I was
giving a reading of my first attempts at translating poems
by József and Ady here in Budapest, I could sense their
success or failure from the audience's reaction to every
line; and this – always chivalrous – ruthlessness, even
though it used to upset me at first, compelled me to face
those very problems which had to be solved if I were not
to bog down. ... Yes, even that finger from a quite different
scene pointing sneeringly at a poem I had written in 1950
and adding the comment: "The whole of the Hitler Youth
still shows up in it!" It was said even more sneeringly, but
the answer was right; I would have liked to cut off his
finger as close as possible to his neck. ... Arrayed in ignominy and shame, that was it. ... He was right; he had
pointed to the very spot: not to a tender spot – you can
find those for yourself – no, to the spot you think is

sound. ... My thanks to him, but shouldn't a friend have pointed it out

And a misdirection, a challenge in the wrong direction, is an inadequate challenge; instead of pointing the way toward the utmost you can do, it bypasses your potential

A statement cannot make a statement about itself. The Cretan who says that all Cretans are liars. The crowd that encompasses itself as an element. Münchhausen pulling himself out of the bog by his own hair. The analogy to this: literature – criticism. But what to call this analogy

Like the leopard, I can't and never would be able to change my spots. But inside that skin: to make the most of it, to have the courage to pursue all its possibilities which, in view of my Bohemian heritage, means the courage to give my imagination free rein, to embrace the baroque, the courage to dream and to accept paradoxes

But isn't that partial function, the one I must fulfill, at odds with all this? Doesn't that demand precision in conforming to reality, as well as objectivity, factualness, credibility

If the leopard could change its spots

"So they came to a river. The little old woman placed Erzsók the Beautiful in the water and stepped on her foot as she grasped the other, and then tore Erzsók the Beautiful in two. And then many toads and frogs and all kinds of other creatures sprang forth from her.

"'You see, my son, they would have done you to death, even if you had possessed a thousand souls!'

"She washed the pieces till they were clean, fitted them one to the other, and they grew together. And now the maiden was a hundred times more beautiful than before. ..."

A Hungarian fairy tale: this motif of liberation by killing, dismembering, or at least causing pain, appears in the fairy tales of all lands. Deliverance by decapitation; deliverance by flaying; deliverance by fire; deliverance by hurling against a wall. It is a human experience

One should think through the Marsyas myth. But where to find its sources

All Saints; All Souls: outside the Church of Saint Francis, in a corner, candles trembling in the wind, a little cluster of candles, and in front of them trembling old men and women, the candles are tall, very slender, trembling angels, more faithful than the faithful

In Ferenc's favorite café, a bit grubby, a bit tarty, I wouldn't have thought that of Ferenc, and Ferenc himself is unrecognizable. I wanted to discuss with him his thesis that the writer should be able to write about anything; I wanted to ask him what it was that inhibited the writer, was it something internal or external, fatness or chains, hurdles on the course or in his breast: the hurdle of shame, the hurdle of guilt, the hurdle of language, the hurdle of theory, the hurdle of practice; I wanted to discuss the relationship between society and taboo and was already picturing myself in the role of defender of the taboo, but Ferenc would have none of it, he is in no mood to argue today, the weather is so beautiful, the air is so clear, and today is All Souls' Day, he feels happy, and he drinks one cognac after another and tells one joke after another and, as if by prearrangement, a colleague of his is suddenly standing in front of us, straight out of the comics: very gaunt, very shabby, big round bulging eyes in his wizened bird-face that wobbles aslant above his gangling body as if suspended from a spine reaching right up to the crown of his head. The bird-headed one raises one finger toward the waitress and looks at Ferenc, and Ferenc nods, and his colleague, as he sits down, asks in German: "Have you heard this one?" The waitress brings him a cognac; "have you heard this one?" asks the bird-headed one, tossing back his cognac, "in Vienna, on the Ring, you know, two Jews, they don't know each other, so these two Jews are walking toward each other in Vienna along the Ring, and one of them says: 'Good morning, the name's Bone,' and the other man says: 'What d'you mean, bone, am I a dog?'" The bird-headed one roars with laughter, tips back the empty glass, Ferenc signals to the waitress, the bird-headed one laughs again and says to me: "Get it, my friend, the joke, I mean? Of course he's not a bone, that fellow Bone, it's just his name, Bone, get it? That's his name, Bone, that's what he's called, and that's why he introduces himself as Bone, and the other fellow says: 'What d'you mean, bone, am I a dog?' and of course he's not a dog, just like the other fellow isn't a bone, but on the other hand he's not called Dog either the way Bone is called Bone, otherwise it wouldn't be a joke, otherwise he would say: 'Pleased to meet you, my name's Dog,' and then the other fellow would say: 'What d'you mean, Dog, I'm not a bone, I'm only *called* Bone,' and then the other fellow says: 'It's just my name too, Dog, but I'm not a dog!' and if the other man says: 'Nor am I,' where's the joke? No dog and no bone, if that's what they're both called – but then he isn't called Dog, get it? That's just the joke, he thinks he's saying bone because he takes him for a dog, but then he can't very well say: 'Good morning, the name's not Bone' when his name *is* Bone, and if the other man asks. 'What d'you mean it's not your name, what *is* your name if you have one?' the other man says: 'It *is* Bone,' so he might as well have said right aways: 'The name's Bone,' get it?" He tosses back the second cognac: "So, Bone," he says, and the waitress looks at me, and I nod. "Bone," he says, "if that fellow was not called Bone but Dog, well, he would have introduced himself as Dog and not as Bone, and if he says – supposing he's called Dog: 'My name's Dog,' the other fellow says: 'What d'you mean, Dog, am I a bone?' That's what the man says who's not called Dog, if the other man's called Dog and not Bone; but if *he* were called Dog he would *say* 'Dog' and they would both shout: 'What d'you mean, am I supposed to be a dog?', in Vienna, on the Ring, two Jews, get it? But he's only *called* Bone, and the other fellow isn't called Dog at all, but not Bone either, he's called Meier, get it? Meier with an i," and he tosses back the third cognac, gets up, says: "But that's not part of the joke, that he's called Meier, only that Bone is called Bone," and gets up, points at me, says: "Gee-Dee-Ar, right?" and tips back the empty glass and sidles out

For God's sake, I ask Ferenc, who was that? and Ferenc says: Bone, of course – you mean to say you don't know Bone

Have you heard this one? Ferenc asks, there's this citizen of the German Democratic Republic who comes to Vienna in his Trabant and parks it and turns off the engine, and then he notices that people are stopping and looking at his car, and more and more arrive, more and more and still more and finally there are a hundred people standing around gaping, and your fellow countryman gets out and is happy to see them all admiring his car, and then someone taps him on the shoulder and says: 'Scuse me, sir, you sure have a nice little car there, did you make it yourself

Have you heard this one, Ferenc, I ask, Moishe reads in the Scriptures: He who is feeble in spirit can trust the Lord not to let him fall, and angels will bear him up on their hands – and Moishe thinks, marvelous, I always did want to jump out of the fourth floor into the courtyard, and jumps from the fourth floor onto the paving, breaks arms and legs, and lies there yelling. Along comes Abram and sees Moishe lying there and asks: For Heaven's sake, Moishe, why are you lying there, what's the matter? and Moishe looks at him and says: Nothing special, Abram, I just found out that I'm wise

Are you wise now? Ferenc asks wordlessly, and I shake my head without moving

Ferenc shows me a secondhand bookstore that I actually didn't know about. "It's a secret," he says, and all the wishful dreams of my list of desiderata No. 3 spring to my mind: Vol. 50/51 of the first edition of Jean Paul's collected works; Vols. 9 and 12 of the collected works of Ludwig Tieck; Lichtenberg's collected works (why not?); Vol. 1 of the Low German fairy tales in the Diederich series that hasn't yet shown up in any of the bookstores at home; Hegel's *Philosophy of Religion*; Jahnn's *Pastor Ephraim Magnus*; Mutzenbacher; Kisch's poems in the Pierson edition; *The Child's Book of Confusion* – but nothing, and worse than nothing: as if to mock me, two copies of the last Joseph Roth which I was still lacking and

that I managed to get hold of in Berlin the day before
I left

And not a single item from my list No. 4 (mythologica

Madách's much-disputed phalanstery scene: the future of
a human race which, since its energy supplies, especially
the sun, are going to be exhausted within the next four
thousand years, has submitted to a purely utilitarian way
of thinking and acknowledges but a single motive for
human behavior: measurable utility. All forces are to be
concentrated on the goal of maximum production and ex-
ploitation of energy; anything that cannot demonstrably
serve this goal is eliminated, e.g., art and philosophy. But
as a result society becomes inhuman four thousand years
before its calculated end and, what's more, inhuman from
every aspect, even the aspect of utility. This utility devoid
of any imagination is in itself totally useless; it is the fos-
silized utility of yesterday in the society of today and tomorrow. Society stagnates and, since in its obtuseness it
extracts the least rather than the greatest possible usefulness, from its members, it deepens the stagnation further
still. Michelangelo has to keep turning out the same chairlegs; Luther controls the temperature of the boiler; Plato
is herding cattle; every marriage is determined by a ridiculous notion of eugenics, and someone making screws
must spend the rest of his life making screws, for – so the
elders believe – thus and only thus would the most perfect
screws in the world be produced. ... Well, it so happens
that that's not how they are produced; the most perfect
screws are produced by machine and, if Plato herds cattle,
Michelangelo turns out chairlegs, and Luther looks after
the boiler, these machines will never be invented. ... What
is needed is the maximum unshackling of imagination, the

leap into a radical Other. ... A society that makes Plato herd cattle instead of developing philosophers from herdsmen is more backward than any herdsman society and deserves to perish, for the controlling power is not even utility but the most conspicuous mark of the bourgeoisie, obtuseness and malice; this bourgeois society has been thought through to its end, even before it has begun, and lo and behold: its final form is the concentration camp

Do what you like, you can't get away from Auschwitz

To retranslate Madách, at least a few scenes, that would be a challenge. In none of the deficient translations have I felt as strongly as I do here that the inadequate form must have altered the content of the German version

Assuming you had been ordered to Auschwitz, what would you have done there? No, don't say the question is meaningless simply because you were not there. ... Granted, a kindly fate saved me during the war (and before too) from committing atrocities; it is no credit to me, I was not ordered to commit them. I was not required to shoot at defenseless people, drive off cattle, set fire to buildings, march off women and children, cut down fruit trees, use torture at interrogations or even to conduct them, nothing of all that. ... But if I had been ordered to

Might I have got to Auschwitz? Certainly: in September 1938, instead of volunteering with K. for the SA I need only have volunteered with W. for the SS, for the Black SS. The question of Hitler Youth, Storm Trooper, or SS was for me merely a question of friendship, nothing else. K. joined the SA, so I joined it too, but I might just as well have followed W. Perhaps I was also put off by the rumor that there was more drill and less free time in the SS, but if W. had supported me in a certain matter I would in return have joined the SS with him. And W. *did* get to Auschwitz

And it needn't have been Auschwitz, just a handful of murders and not even in the war, just in the *Kristallnacht*, and not even a handful – just one

And wasn't I disappointed that as Storm Troopers we never saw the "action" we longed for: no fighting, no battles in meeting halls, no border provocations, no penetration of mysterious underworlds where the enemy lurked with pistols and blackjacks, nothing of all that, nothing but marching around through the streets and bellowing songs and rattling collection boxes for the Winter Aid program and everlasting drill and pelting each other with lumps of mud in simulated war games

Just like W., like hundreds of thousands of my kind, I was a young Fascist, thought, felt, dreamed and acted as they did and in Auschwitz I would have done exactly the same as the others and would have called it "my duty

No, don't try and persuade yourself that two and two don't make five, that it is unwarranted to draw conclusions from something that never happened

In Auschwitz you would have functioned at the gas chamber exactly as you did in Kharkov or Athens at your telegraph instrument: that's what you were there for, my friend

"But I would never have killed a child. ..." You see yourself standing in front of the oven with a grand gesture, refusing to carry out an order and throwing yourself into the flames. ... That's how twelve-year-olds dream of heroic deeds. ... True: if your major had summoned you from your telegraph instrument and led you to a child playing on the street and ordered you to kill it with a spade, you wouldn't have done it, but then that's something no one else would have done, obviously W. wouldn't have done it either, but that wasn't the way things happened in Auschwitz, it didn't start like that in Auschwitz, nor did it start like that for W.

Very well then: you weren't there, so you didn't have a chance to be a hero and throw yourself into the flames. ... You did something else: you kept Auschwitz going. By doing my duty so conscientiously and gallantly behind my telegraph instrument, I was doing exactly what was demanded of me and my kind to make Auschwitz work, and we did it the way they wanted us to. ... Not everyone was *required* to gas children

Not every reserve gets sent into battle, but it is a reserve just because it can at any time be sent out to butcher

Was there anything special about you? There is nothing, nothing at all to indicate that you differed from your fellowmen in a way that would have compelled you to behave differently from the others at Auschwitz. And if indeed you had been what was called "soft," you would have condemned your softness and worked at becoming hard

Someone asserts: "I was a young Fascist," and he believes and interprets his belief as follows: "I was young, I was ardent, I was enthusiastic, I was impassioned, I was ready to make sacrifices, to give my all, I was filled with devotion to Fatherland, nation and honor, I was a believer, I was brave, I was obedient, in short: I was all that, but as for what makes a Fascist a Fascist, that I never was when I was a Fascist

One or the other: either you were a Fascist, in which case you would have been a Fascist in Auschwitz too. Or you were not, in which case answer for having supported Fascism in the first place. Or you were a third thing, in which case you were one of those lukewarm ones whom the Lord spits forth from His mouth

And those lukewarm ones would also have killed the child on the street

In that "Not me! – Never me!" humanity shudders within you, and its shudder is also your best part. But that alone won't get you any farther, for that shudder does not include you

In that "Not me! – Never me!" is the howling voice of the Other to say that he was never this One, and indeed in *this* form he never was this One. Without that "Not me!" the Other could not live; but with that "Not me!" he cannot acknowledge the One and hence not come to terms with him

That "Not me! – Never me!" is a basic human right, and anyone who never stammered it would be a stone. But what also lives on in that "Not me! – Never me!" is the romantic concept of the spiritually and morally sovereign individual, and that does not suffice to encompass the movements of our century. ... The meaning of Fascism is not that somewhere there is smoke smelling of human

flesh but that those doing the gassing are interchangeable

"Never me!" – that was also the attitude of that chronicler
of the great Béla, and of all those who read with a shudder
of contempt about the woman who devoured her own feet

How could I ever say that I had come to terms with my
past if I accept chance, which has reigned over it so merci-
fully, to be my supreme arbitrator? Coming to terms with
the past means questioning every possibility, hence also the
most remote

"To understand all is to forgive all" is a phrase used by
those who do not know the difference between understanding and empathy and are neither the One nor the Other
involved in the case in question. They are equally not
qualified to be historians or judges

Hence an equals sign between you and Kaduk, that medi-
cal orderly of Auschwitz? Yes. The degree of guilt is a
juridical question, but let your insight proclaim: You too
could have become Kaduk. ... You did not murder under
Fascism, you were not sentenced to death (which might
also have happened and *also* been just and, moreover,
what you had expected), but you were forced to condemn
to death the person you were, otherwise you could not
have gone on living. Your change started the moment you
began to grasp the fact that Nuremberg was your concern
and not the concern of some – what was the name? –
Göring or Hitler

But how does one carry out one's own execution? At the
window crossbar, a jump from a stool to just above the

floor (undertaken by many, in the latrine of the antifascist school, above the pit, with a note pinned to their chest) would extinguish both, the One as well as the Other. ... The One has the Other by the throat, and the plunge from the church tower would mean the worst possible change. ... Only the Other can conquer the One, and this is no mere act of cognition, it does not happen on this day and at this hour, as it did to Saul on the road to Damascus, and even he sat for three days blind without eating and without drinking. ... Only the Other can conquer the One, the Other who grows out of the One, and he conquers by suffering the process of dying to the One and becoming the Other. ... It is the unity of contradiction, and the change is that process in which contradiction is dissolved – into what? Into the new

That contradiction determines the partial function the fulfilling of which would be your first and foremost duty

Like thousands of others of my generation, I came to Socialism not via the proletarian class struggle or starting from Marxist theory: I arrived at that different social order via Auschwitz. This is what distinguishes my generation from those before and after it, and it is this difference which determines our tasks in literature. ... I shall never escape the past, not even in a Utopia. ... Here too, like the leopard, I cannot change my spots, but I can do what is denied to someone who does not have those spots: I can exhaust all the possibilities of this condition, including the most extreme, the most horrible and the most consoling, and this is something I have hardly even begun

The new social order was the Other as distinguished from Auschwitz; I arrived at it via the gas chambers and had regarded my change as completed when, my will extinguished, I offered myself as a tool to the new social order, instead of being one of its shapers with a contribution which only I could make. All this was contained in that poem pointed to by the sneerer; a bad poem, for all it said was that I was still looking at the new society with my old eyes. I was as far as ever from understanding Socialism as a community in which the free development of each individual is the prerequisite for the free development of all. But this could not be the end, it could only be the beginning of the change

Noise on the street; noise through the open window; mating cries, rutting, gurgling, drunken; in the house across the way, all the shutters go up; laughing, grinning, guffawing, giggling faces behind the panes, and in Líliom's room two young women stand by the open window and wave to the invisible caller. He must live one floor below me, but there is a projecting ledge, and I can't see him, I can only hear him calling: "Come!" he gurgles, "come woman! O woman, come!" and the women, both blonde, curvaceous and slim, long pants and mini-skirt, yellow shirt and blue blouse, laugh as they wave down toward the lust; sirens, they reach out their arms in desire and entice with cupped, beckoning hands, nod, point to themselves and each other, platinum-blonde yellow, platinum-blonde blue, their eyes flash, they blow down a kiss, and now Líliom appears, Líliom in a red sports shirt and leans on the shoulders of the two women, and Líliom laughs, and the air is laughter and the scent of women, the lane laughs, and the blondes open the top button of each other's blouse and shirt, and everywhere there is now light, bright, laughing, laughing light, a laughing lane, a lane filled with high spirits, a lane filled with folly, and Yellow purses her lips, and Blue snaps her fingers, and Red grabs each of them by the hair and pulls back their heads and kisses both, and below there is a roar, a roar of lust that cracks the voice, and silence, and Yellow and Blue and Red and the house across the way laugh uproariously and laugh and clap their hands and hold their sides and laugh and point down toward the window that is silent and that I cannot see; past the yellow moon flies Marguerite, and the curtains begin to close on the laughter; the faces disappear, the lights go out; Líliom lets down the shutters, and one of them catches and remains at an angle to the windowsill, Mallarmé's fan, subdued light behind it, and silence, and then Blue flits past, and then nothing more

Up very early; finished off the *Rebellious Christ* at dawn and once more went through *Nagyon fáj* and the Füst poems in preparation for the reading. Then, taking along the supple, one-volume Hendel edition of Grimms' fairy tales which, for the sake of something to buy on my first visit, I acquired for a few forints in the little antiquarian bookstore in Szeged, out into the mild day somewhere down toward the Danube

Transformation in fairy tales – how strange that the hero usually acts merely as a catalyst. Although he passes through the animal form, he remains essentially unchanged; he may become "even handsomer," "even purer," "even stronger," but this is an embellishment to enable him to participate in the deliverance he brings. But his environment, his social entity (family, castle, country, kingdom) do change, they are rid of a curse, liberated from a calamity

They change, but they are not transformed, they return to their origins. "A" by way of "minus A" becomes "A" again, and everything is exactly as before, an empty process

(According to Engels, the negation of the negation goes from plus A via minus A to A^2 with the square roots of plus A *and* minus A. The negation of the negation is more than the simple position, and from now on and forever it also contains the negation; quadratic equations have *two* roots

and quadratic equations are merely two-dimensional

Idyll – interference – idyll – why is this movement bearable in a fairy tale? Because we look for it in life and hence want to find it in a fairy tale. But if a fairy tale were no more than that, it would be flat. What is really spellbinding in a fairy tale shimmers beneath this movement

One thing is terrible: that the hero brings nothing back from his journeyings into the other world, no memory, no knowledge of what it is to be the Other, no experience. It was a passage, nothing more, and that is dreadful, for it is without consolation, without hope

For he *was* a bear (a horse, a tiger, a stag, a fish, a lion, a hare, a flower, a tree, a stone, a pool), or did he only have the shape of these creatures

And if he was a raven: doesn't he sometimes long to be able to fly

"I am under a spell" – why do we perceive this formula as more or less positive? In ninety-nine cases out of a hundred it was the most frightful thing that could happen

It is not the magic that is unreal in a fairy tale; anyone can learn a bit of witchcraft. ... What makes it a fairy tale is the virtually unlimited potential for communication of all with all, regardless of direction and the restoration of the idyll, the happy ending, the laughter that ends the Western. The fairy tale can fit into reality, but reality cannot fit into the fairy tale

What we read into fairy tales: did the tellers of fairy tales put it there? Hardly; they told fairy tales. But the myths, even as fragments, have retained their power in the fairy tale

And the audience listened to the fairy tale and heard it
murmur: This tale concerns you

and this is exactly how, after Nuremberg and Auschwitz,
I perceived fairy tales: *tua res agitur*; and I had been
shocked to think that in my hands was a book containing
the essence of German history, and I had been looking at it
a hundred times, just as the people had looked at the
swineherd a hundred times without suspecting that deliverance would come through him

Once upon a time —
>*tua res agitur*

**The next day, when she had taken her place at
table with the King and all his courtiers and was
eating from her little golden dish, there was a splish
splash, splish splash, something crawling up the
marble staircase, and on reaching the top it knocked
at the door and called out: Princess, youngest
daughter of the King, open up to me! She ran to see
who was there, but when she opened the door she
saw the frog sitting outside it. Whereupon she
hastily slammed the door shut, resumed her place at
table, and was full of fear —**
>*tua res agitur*

They are such strange names, they make me wonder
>*tua res agitur*

**Hardly had the dog run a few steps when it stood
before a deep pool and could go no farther, and a
naked arm reached up out of the water, seized the
dog and dragged it down. On seeing this the**

huntsman went back to fetch three men and he made
them bring pails and scoop out the water. When they
could see to the bottom they saw a wild man lying
there, brown of body like rusty iron —

tua res agitur

Then the father went to the girl and said: My child,
if I don't cut off both your hands the Devil will take
me, and in my fear I promised him. Help me in my
plight, and forgive me the evil I do to you —

tua res agitur

I smell, smell human flesh —

tua res agitur

I dreamed that in a certain kingdom there stood an
apple tree that used to bear golden apples and now
would not even put forth leaves. What could be the
reason? Hey, if they only knew! replied the Devil.
There is a mouse nibbling at the roots; if they kill it,
the tree will once again bear golden apples, but if the
mouse continues to nibble the tree will wither away

tua res agitur

If you will speak the truth and confess that you have
unlocked the forbidden door, I will open your mouth
and restore your speech —

tua res agitur

We bring with us not only the golden bird, they said,
we have also captured the golden horse and the
maiden of the golden castle. There was great
rejoicing, but the horse would not eat, the bird
would not whistle, and the maiden sat and wept —

When Katy-Liz awoke after a long sleep, she stood
there half naked and said to herself: Is it I, or is it
not I? Alas, it is not I! —
tua res agitur

and nigh on seven years had passed and they
rejoiced and believed they would soon be delivered
and were yet so far from it —
tua res agitur

Then the peasants were amazed and said: Little man,
where do you come from? Do you come from the
water? — Indeed, the little man replied, I sank deep,
deep down till at last I came to the bottom —
tua res agitur

Wherever have you been? — Ah, Father, I have been
in a mousehole, in a cow's belly, and in a wolf's
stomach; now I mean to stay with you —
tua res agitur

Yet fairy tales contain only fragments of myths

Although: *how* polished, and in *what* a setting

From the café emerges an elderly, sourfaced, liverish-look-
ing gentleman wearing a close-fitting brown velvet jacket and
a brown velvet cap; his body looks pinched – no, rather more
compressed, his left shoulder into his right breast and his
right shoulder into his left breast, with his left shoulder
slightly lower than the right. He gives a pained smile in all
directions, and at that moment a little round man enters

through the revolving door who, as soon as he is in the lobby, looks back again toward the street and, in doing so, he swivels his torso a hundred and eighty degrees in his hips, simultaneously bending the middle of the twisted torso to one side – a movement unfolding in time as reflected in three-dimensional space. The compressed one passes him with a nod, and from an armchair rises an old man with bushy eyebrows and a vertically telescoped body but no hump. ... The three men stand in a group; it is – well, what? – fantastic. The word is overused, but I can't think of any other, and the bushy one raises his shoulder above his ear, and now I've got it: cubistic, at last I understand cubism, and even the liverish one's progress toward the revolving door is cubistic, a kind of parallelogram of forces, two divergent tendencies resulting in a final central axis. He walks straight ahead, in an absolutely straight line but straight ahead as the center of a constant thrust to left and right, and the round one swivels back again and toward the man with the bushy eyebrows who, stretching out his arms and embracing the round one, shifts his body diagonally against itself

The day before yesterday a Hungarian, Professor Gábor, was awarded the Nobel Prize for holography, for a process by which three-dimensional images can be developed from two-dimensional ones – is there also such a thing for developing four-dimensional ones from three-dimensional ones

How many dimensions do we need to avoid ambiguity anyway? I can represent a three-dimensional object unambiguously on a two-dimensional plane so that it can be unambiguously reconstructed, but I cannot represent the two-dimensional plane in the one-dimensional line: the Other is lacking

If I can represent a four-dimensional object unambiguously in three dimensions and in turn a three-dimensional object unambiguously in two dimensions, doesn't that make the three-dimensional superfluous? Certainly – but only where the representation appears: on paper

Is everything two-dimensional always a representation of the spatial, or are there such things as pure planes? Despite all efforts, painting has not been able to eliminate space. The fairy tale is two-dimensional, but one is always aware of the depth of the abyss. On the other hand the flat, the shallow, that makes a pretense at depth – could one pinpoint the difference, is there a method for this, is even the terminology correct? What do we mean when we speak of the "two-dimensional" in literature? What are its dimensions, what is the X, the Y, the Z axis? Why do we call that poem shallow and this one deep? What is the difference between "too long" and "too broad"? How does time figure in these coordinates

Depth, too, is only one dimension; it must join a plane in order to yield three dimensions. By itself, it is merely a direction. ... Depth and width, too, or depth and length, yield only two dimensions

Fairy stories are two-dimensional, but they point toward depth. In so doing, they point beyond themselves

He who travels in one direction only, without interruption, enters the void

Fairy tales had been my lyrical concept; for many years now, that concept has been exhausted, yet, rather than detach myself from them, I have continued to consult them

To advance from two dimensions to three means to change direction

Myths are the experiences of mankind; fairy tales represent the refining of myth-motives. Myth draws upon full reality, the fairy tale on fragments of myths. Myth is firsthand, fairy tale secondhand. Nevertheless, determinant traits of life are visible in the fairy tale, as distinct from some literature which calls itself realistic but is merely paper

Fairy tales are kaleidoscopic images of myth-splinters: multicolored, single-faceted, enchanting and interchangeable

The fairy tale points to abysses, the myth *is* abysmal

In the myth, humans, like gods, are whole, uncrippled creatures. In the fairy tale, humans are shadow-creatures, and the spirits are hypertrophications of these shadows, but of the same dimensionality. This is why – something unthinkable in myth – each can communicate with each in any way or direction he pleases. Whoever rubs Aladdin's lamp is served by the genie; in the myth, not everyone is free to touch the lamp, let alone for the genie to appear to him

In the fairy tale we may find automatic dispensers of miracles; in the myth, strictly speaking, neither automatic dispensers nor miracles

In the myth, humans and gods are the Other for each other, and the one cannot be expressed by the other; nor is the one its antithesis. The fairy tale knows only bipolar opposites, and the evil one is the exact opposite of the hero, matter and anti-matter, plus A and minus A. At best there are intermediate steps, gradations, incompleteness, but gradations only within a scale. Myth is multidimensional

Fairy tales, like myths, are related to games, except that in fairy tales there is only one set of game rules, and these are unequivocal and invariably adhered to. Myth knows various systems of game rules, those for humans and those for gods, and to each side those of the other are neither completely clear nor completely identifiable

In the fairy tale, unequivocal justice is the rule; in the myth, there are varieties of justice

The fairy tale teaches us to dream; the myth teaches us to live. The fairy tale provides consolation; the myth, experience

"The myth is devoid of all wishful thinking" – these words in a letter to me are a key. Fairy tales are wish-dreams on a myth-basis

Fairy tales are lines on a plane; myths are movements in space

The myth is never, the fairy tale always, fatalistic, hence it admits no alternative. The happy ending is certain, indeed unavoidable, and one or two exceptions prove the rule – a Hungarian fairy tale, for example, in which the miraculous little ox with the detachable horn must die. Barbara was so upset when I read it to her that she wept, and I wanted to bring the little ox to life again, but she didn't believe me even when I turned the page and put my finger on an imaginary resuscitation. She did not trust my efforts to console her; something had touched her that was more and more terrible than the twenty-four-headed dragon: life

We have become used to associating the idea of fatalism with that of pessimism, but in fact there is also a thoroughly optimistic form of fatalistic thinking. Brecht's words that Socialism is as good or as bad as we make it is a warning against precisely this fatal belief in automation

In the fairy tale, morality is mechanized; in myth it is created

Myths are processes, fairy tales results

In the fairy tale, the good character (who is always the hero) always triumphs; in myth, the gods are not invincible

As a teller of myths of the highest rank, Anna Seghers lives on in our midst with her complete works. Her "Peasants of Hrushovo" are the song of another Iliad; her Argonauts sail to Mexico and Haiti; what happens in Mrs. Kamptschik's apartment during the setting up of a machine gun belongs in a new volume of *Metamorphoses*, and *The Man and His Name*, despite some flaws, tells a story of an Odysseus of our time

We block our own path toward understanding myths if we confuse mythical with mystical. The mythical element is that which raises realism above naturalism, and creating above mere illustrating. This distinction is not contingent upon a particular theme – say, a political one. It is from

Seghers that we can learn how such an eminently political phenomenon as the Party line can be experienced in literary terms

Here I sense an approach to my problem of shame and shamelessness. In the myth, the whole human being is always present, even as a sexual creature, even as a natural creature, but never reduced to these. For such reductions are merely the reverse of narrow-minded prudishness, not its overcoming and hence no less narrow-minded. To state, for instance, that man must defecate is not to disseminate a human experience, and to depict this act not a sign of literary courage; but that Saul, wanting to relieve himself, has to enter David's cave and is now in the hands of his enemy, and that his foe/friend cuts off a corner of his robe during this act is a piece of great myth that could not have happened in any other place or any other way

It is high time for me to correct a line: "The hero is always afraid."

It occurs in one of my fairy-tale poems, and here I am guilty of unduly generalizing a feature of a Romanian fairy tale about a battle with a dragon. ... This feature had overwhelmed me; it was exactly what I was looking for in fairy tales and, seizing upon it, I hoped to find it confirmed in other fairy tales. It wasn't; in all other fairy tales the hero is *never* afraid, for fear dwells in that dimension which has been left out

Silly though it may sound: I sometimes worried about having to go away without having made this correction, but the occasion never arose

The difference between fairy tale and myth is the difference between understanding and empathy. The fairy tale makes complete sense in terms of explanation, but it cannot arouse empathy except in daydreams. Myths are as far from making complete sense in rational terms as is a work of art, but they are occurring all the time, and anyone able to see them and narrate them is a poet

Dialectics in the fairy tale are a reflection of the dialectics of the myth: the result of dialectics, not dialectics as a process. Myths happen; fairy tales are the finished product that never happened

(Later at Gábor's looked up Thomas Mann's well-known utterance: "During recent decades, myth has been too often misused as an instrument of obscurantist counterrevolution for a mythic novel like *Joseph* not to have aroused the suspicion, when it first appeared, that its author was swimming along with the same murky current. This suspicion had to be dropped, for closer scrutiny revealed that the function of myth had been transformed in a way that had not been thought possible. A process was being observed comparable to that of a cannon captured in battle being turned around and aimed at the enemy. In that book, myth was taken out of the hands of Fascism and *humanized* throughout the very farthest reaches of language, if posterity should find anything noteworthy about it, it will be this."

And a little farther on, in the same address, these words about men "whose identity was open behind them to receive things past. ..."

In fairy tales all things are interchangeable, in myths nothing; myth is a process into which nothing can be inserted but from which nothing can be cut out either. Myths can, to be sure, intersect, they can also intertwine, just as Aeschylus intertwined Io and Prometheus, but a portion of Prometheus cannot be interchanged with a portion of Io, though a portion of Aladdin is interchangeable with a portion of Ali Baba

For this reason the people in fairy tales cannot change either, they can merely be put under or released from a spell or turned into the moral opposite. A turns, via minus A, back into A, or minus A becomes plus A. These switches into the opposite occur simply by the exchanging of attributes. In myth, however, the dialectics of change and identity prevail which I sought for in vain in fairy tales

The Soviet fairy-tale dramatists such as Yevgeni Schwarz, Paustovski, Olesha, have led the fairy tale back to the myth. *The Shadow*, *The Ordinary Miracle*, *The Dragon*, *The Little Iron Ring*, *The Three Fatbellies*, are, despite their designation, myths, not fairy tales, hence their impact

And vice versa: the tellers of synthetic fairy tales have reduced the fairy tale from two dimensions to one; they have drawn their products from the fragments and splinters of traditional fairy tales, they are third hand, and what you get from that is hackneyed. All trace of myth has gone from it, and consequently all trace of life

From fairy tale to myth signifies: to the full life, to the whole man, to dialectical reality

Reading; certainty: the Füst translations can stand. If this audience approves, it is so. But my approach to *Nagyon fáj* is wrong and unsuccessful. József's poem contains elements of the gruesome and the grotesque which I have failed to express

Wonder whether I shall find the strength to tackle Ady again

And which of us knows what Petőfi is

Long walk in the evening with Zoltán and Ferenc, and only now do I discover, during a conversation about *Nagyvilág*, the journal for world literature, that Zoltán has translated Hermlin's "Scardanelli"

Flowers and stars in the river, and seen from one point, only one, a fiery wheel

Ferenc quotes Hölderlin

An espresso; colleagues; long discussions about translation and the difficulties of both languages; I complain that in German there is no rhyme for that most important word *Mensch*, and Ágnes deplores the dreary sound of the word for "love": three horrible, short, empty "e"'s – *szerelem*, taddadum, the sound of a toy trumpet

Ferenc talks about a young gypsy poet; he calls him Hungary's greatest lyric hope. ... I shall never learn Hungarian

I have been unjust to fairy tales; I compared them with the myth in only one, although essential, aspect. But fairy tales are often jewels, myths merely rough diamonds

Across the way, all shutters closed

The slogan of the popular heroes of Hungarian fairy tales:
We'll manage somehow!

Very well, my little fellow, said the King, but look: here are ninety-nine human heads impaled on posts, and your head will be the hundredth if you can't hide yourself properly!
   The little swineherd refused to be intimidated, saying merely: We'll manage somehow.

I would be glad to take you in, but there isn't even a corner in our house where you could lie down, we have so many children.
   Never mind, replied the two travelers, we'll lie on the ground on a bit of straw.
   Very well, said the poor man, if you're satisfied with that! But that's not the only trouble. My wife is expecting a child at any moment. Where would we put you then?
   We'll manage somehow, said the two travelers.

It is the quintessence of a people's experience. ... German fairy tales know no such formula

November 3

Dream:

I am lying on my couch looking at the window and its familiar red curtain, and I think: Let it be green now! In a dream you can do anything. The curtain instantly turns green. I laugh and gaily say: Now blue! Now yellow! Now black!, and it works every time. I sit up and say: And now red with green dots!, and behold it works again! I give some thought to my next wish, and I can't think of anything more, and then the curtain dissolves. I hurry to the window; the curtain has disappeared, the window is open, and as I look down a truck drives up covered with a tarpaulin. The truck stops; I sense a deadly danger, and through the tarpaulin rise two battered men, murmuring inaudibly, their bleeding red-brown bodies painted with egg yolk between the shoulders and on the hips. I try to draw back but find I can't move; the men slowly raise their heads, and on seeing the intact, round eyeballs in the flayed face muscles I scream and wake up screaming

My morning's reading: Hungarian syntax, which goes backward like the clock on the Altneu synagogue in Prague, continues to obsess me

How can a language, which is sequential, express the simultaneous? "I look toward the door and simultaneously hear the telephone." In spite of the "simultaneously," this sentence suggests a sequence: I saw the door, recognized it as a door, and at that instant, while still in the process of looking but after completing the recognition, I heard the telephone ring. In certain cases this sequence would even suggest a causal connection: "I look toward the door and simultaneously remember N. N." Here, once again, despite the "simultaneously," the springing up of the name is a result of the look toward the door: probably, so the reader thinks, there had been some incident with a door (unexpected visit; getting thrown out; a sudden knock or whatever) that produced a certain memory-algorism.

The best way of grasping the time-relationship is when I form two sentences each with its own subject and then combine them: "I look toward the door. Simultaneously the telephone rings." – "I look, and the telephone rings, toward the door." This sentence verges on simultaneity. I could also say: "I see, and the telephone rings, the door," but this sentence does not convey that I am looking toward the door, i.e., moving my head. What a bind

Interesting that, in gaining time-accuracy, I have to sacrifice what was formerly the common subject: "I look, and hear the telephone, toward the door" – this sentence is utter confusion

Also interesting, although not entirely unexpected, that the moment simultaneity is even approximately achieved, the word "simultaneously" becomes superfluous, in fact an intrusion

The telephone is Ferenc; he wants to take me out for a browse around the stores

My last day, and I should be making use of it to catch up on notes for my travel sketches, the new Metro for example, the synagogue, the Ring, i.e., the heterogenous parts of the Great and Little Ring which, each being entirely different from the other, define three worlds within Pest –

but by now I have come to take this city so much for granted that there is nothing more for me to note, unless I write down everything. In front of the hotel, for instance: the little passage, its concrete pillars, their number, their shape, their arrangement, their shadows on the concrete surface of the floor, its structure, the marks on it, the imprinted ones and the transient ones, its dirt, its slope toward the sidewalk, its merging with the sidewalk, all the soles stepping on it, all the shoes, all the feet, walking, stepping, standing; the bistro in the corner of the passage, its menu displayed outside in a kind of peep show, its frame, its glass; the list of dishes, the typewriter type, the condition of the ribbon, the two signatures, the names (surname, first name), the handwriting, its characteristics, the position of the names on the menu, the ranks of the signers, the manner in which the menu is attached in the display; the display box of the night club with its seven photos, and each photo in its totality and each photo in every detail, the positions of the photos in relation to each other and their overall positioning in the frame, the frame, the position of the frame in relation to the peep-show frame, the surface between the two, the shape of this surface, the night-club poster, its lettering, its words, their meaning, their type, the attachment of the poster to the wall and the position of the poster in relation to the photo display and the wall and the angle of the wall and the wall and the menu frame and the view into the bistro through the big glass pane; the big glass pane, its dimensions, its material, its framing and the grooves between it and the framing, the marks on the glass, the marks of fingers, the marks of flies, the marks of rags, the marks of newspaper, the traces of dust, the traces of soot, the curtains at the sides of the glass pane, the awning above the pane, the mechanism to open or shut the awning, its struts, its framework, its ring

for the hook on the pole to pull it up; the counter, the glass
and the chrome and the brass of the counter, the sandwiches, the top row of sandwiches, the bottom row of sandwiches, one sandwich, each sandwich with its filling and
the size and shape of the filling, and the relative positions
of the ingredients, the cakes, the pies, the candy, the packages of cigarettes, the packages of cigars, the boxes of
matches, the beer tap, the taps for yellow and pink lemonade, the drop hanging from a tap, the pipe, its bend, the
bolt, its screws; the soda-water bottles in the sink, the
cognac bottles, the liqueur bottles, the wine bottles, the
sink, the taps for the sink, the brush for the sink, the
bubbles in the sink, the swirl in the sink, the glasses in the
sink, the hands in the sink, the dirt in the sink, the glasses
beside the sink, the glasses below the bottom row of sandwiches, the glasses in the glass cabinet, the glass cabinet,
the various shelves of the glass cabinet, the coffee machine,
the coffee machine in its parts, the coffee machine in its
relative position to the counter and to the glass cabinet behind and the cash register in front; the counter girl, her
little cap, her hair style, her face, her age, her smile, the
weariness of her smile, the signs of the weariness of her
smile in the corners of her mouth and eyes, the change in
her smile as the customers change at her counter, the
change in the degree of the smile, the nature of the smile,
the indications of these changes in her face, the difference
of these differences in the corners of her mouth and eyes;
the cash register; the cashier; the girl making coffee, and
the little caps worn by each, the hair styles of each, the
faces of each, the smiles of each, the different nature of the
smiles of each, the signs of this in their faces; the tables;
the chairs; the stand-up tables, the shape of the stand-up
tables, the legs of the stand-up tables, the fastenings of
the legs of the stand-up tables in the floor; the floor as a

whole; the corners of the floor; the baseboard around the
floor under each wall and in each corner; the floor under
each stand-up table; the tops of the stand-up tables, the
glasses and plates and ashtrays and cutlery on each stand-
up table, their shape, their contents; the walls; the pic-
tures; the ceiling; the air; the door; the inscriptions on the
toilet doors; the symbols on the toilet doors; the other pane
of glass; the lamps; the pedestal ashtrays; the signs on the
walls; the signs on the counter; the sign at the cash register; the price tags; the coathooks, the coatstand; the
coats, each individual one and their totality; the customers,
their number: nineteen, no, seventeen, no, twenty-two,
their clothes, their expressions, their bodies, their gestures,
their walk, the way they eat, the way they drink, the way
they stand in line, the way they pay, the way they speak,
the way they flirt, the way they smoke; the way of attract-
ing, the attempts at petting, the style, the character, the
nature, the language, the personality in their totality,
twenty-two, twenty-one variations in the one bistro out of
four hundred bistros in Budapest at seven minutes after
nine in the morning of the third of November in the year
one thousand nine hundred and seventy-one Anno Do-
mini, and now twenty-three customers, now twenty-four,
the shapeless market woman, the little man with the folded
briefcase under his arm, the plump girl in the crushed-vinyl
coat and black mini-skirt above the much too tight panties,
the happy, unshaven soldier, the two mutton-chopped
Germans eating anchovy eggs while discussing street
theater, the two flies on the windowpane listening in on
them, the newspaper rack inside; the newsstand outside,
the newspapers, the newsvendor, his cashbox, the coins
and bills in his cashbox, his customers, me, the passers-by,
all those passing through the passage turning to the left of
the passage to the right of the passage into the depths of

the Metro with the ascending and descending tide of humanity and the piercing voice of the mute girl selling speckled corn-on-the-cob in the tide that rises and plunges through marble springs canals cables bubbles mud rocks to the bottom of the Metro over concrete steel rocks mud cables canals filth graves ruins rubble bubbles rock lava magma fire exploding nuclei

everything eludes you

Nibbling a corncob, Ferenc emerges from the Metro; drifting toward Váci utca in twelve different smells of smoke: of chestnuts; of coffee; of coal; of gas; of wood; of gasoline; of iron; of earth; of the Danube; of sausage; of tobacco; a haze woven into the day; ships and hills; the triumphant white of the bridge gateway and in that one section of the street one millionth of all the people in the world

Barbara had asked me to bring back some black frames for her; I remembered them as being dirt-cheap, but they are much more expensive than at home. Surprisingly cheap and beautiful, on the other hand, were some wall plates, handmade individual pieces copied from famous museum specimens; also very reasonable are the plated replicas of Scythian jewelry adapted to clasps, brooches, pendants, cufflinks, rings, bracelets, all to be found in an almost empty store ten steps beyond Vörösmarty Square with its crowds of bargain-hunting foreigners, yet a stranger would never think of taking those extra ten steps

The courtyard of an old building in Pest painted a wonderfully fresh white, the carpet-beating rack a work of art: a very thick, smooth rod of dark golden-brown wood resting on smooth black iron supports protruding from the rough wall and curving gently upward

A garden gate in Louis Seize design smiles resignedly outside a baroque church

Narrow, six-story lanes, dim, severe school corridors but the courtyards like bowers framed by arches and the mild, flesh-colored air in the open passageways

Attila's horsemen wearing berets

A tiny café, no larger than a niche in the wall, a smile in the façade

Huge flat baskets full of rosebuds

The monklike church in the chuckling of the lanes

Cheese wheels

Clusters of turquoise grapes

A gypsy child talking to a soldier

A man in a black suit pumping his bicycle

Black pitchers and black plates

Inverted classicism

The sacrificing of Isaac

Geranium windowsills

Blaspheming saints disembodied on the air

Scent of lovage

Window gables like magicians' hats

A bashful tobacco store

Lanterns for barricades

Mailboxes like coaches

A waiter in shirtsleeves

Rosary hands

Flapping laundry

Cats and spinning tops

We stroll along, Ferenc chatting away, when suddenly a
third person is walking beside us, walking a few steps invisibly, and I know it is Apollyon. A gray shadow, shapeless against the gray wall, a breath of cold, a bitter smile,
and half a lifetime is long since past. Justify also what you
have not written! In the fairy tale about lost time, a fairy
collected all the wasted time, and the end begins with the
abundance of the beginning, but here Apollyon grins and
displays his cupped, shadow-filled hands; lost, irretrievably lost time. Moving away from the fairy tale means
changing direction, but do I still have the strength for that?
Changing the dimension means neither forward nor back,
it means what it says: into the Other. ... The wall is bare,
the shadow has disappeared; sun; children, chestnuts;

roses; Ferenc telling about Pest's Old City, about Calvin Square and Henszlmann Lane and Magyar utca with its famous bordellos and the famous Krúdy Gyula and his whores and his duels and his feasts and his end in excrement and wine and about the fantastic books of his experiences, and Ferenc goes on and on, and I nod and ask questions, and we stroll: courtyards, squares, arcades, a garden, the Museum of Literature, the laboratory of Molnár és Moser, the most exquisite perfume laboratory in Budapest, a little farther on Heckenast's printing works where Stifter's stories were published, Thomas Mann's hotel, one of Ady's bistros, one of Babits' cafés, someone walks past us and someone walks toward us, past and toward, toward, toward, past, and someone stops, and a voice says bitterly: "He doesn't recognize me," and: "Professor K.!" I exclaim, "Professor K., of course, what a pleasure, Professor, forgive me, how could I ever forget our discussion last year in the gallery of the Astoria above the fighting bronze centaurs, down in the lobby stood the turquoise-blue gentleman from Luxembourg with the eight huge yellow pigskin suitcases, shouting that the ninth one was missing, and we talked about Madách and about surrealism and about the Psalms," and K. smiles benevolently as usual, and tells me he still hasn't moved, after eleven years, although for eleven years water has been coming through the ceiling and for eleven years his books have been packed in boxes, but then it's just as easy to work in a café, in the library, while walking, everywhere, always, and then the fish soup in the bistro is hot and spicy, and K. asks what I'm doing these days, and I shrug my shoulders, and K. smiles benevolently, the fish soup couldn't be better, Apollyon is with Marguerite, there is no smell of sulphur, and the baked butter noodles with cottage cheese and pork crackling are delicious, and the waiter laughs and charges us for a salad he hasn't served, and then we all laugh, a pleasant lunch hour, a cheerful good-bye, and in a few weeks I shall be fifty, and that's all there is, and it is slowly getting colder

In the afternoon, a long talk with A. G., and the view over the river and over the hills

The allegory of digging a pit: hope

That evening with Ferenc at a night club; boring; stupid; fled. Still fuming, improvised a nice little hermit's game: taking apart suitable sayings (condition: whole sentences with no subsidiary clauses, subject in the singular only, no relative pronoun) so that you have the subject here and the predicate there, then writing down each part on the front and back of a filing card, shuffling the cards and then drawing two cards and putting two random half-sayings together – and this is what happens:

An apple a day is no vice
Poverty keeps the doctor away

The early bird sometimes nods
Homer catches the worm

Misery is in the eye of the beholder
Beauty makes strange bedfellows

One picture does not make a spring
One swallow is better than a thousand words

Honesty never won fair lady
Faint heart is the best policy

Hunger is in the eating
The proof of the pudding is the best sauce

A rolling stone goes a long way
A little kindness gathers no moss

Half a loaf is another man's poison
One man's meat is better than no bread

The love of money is good for the soul
Confession is the root of all evil

Money turneth away wrath
A soft answer begets money

A stitch in time is a penny gained
A penny saved saves nine

A new broom drives out good
Bad money sweeps clean

Virtue is but skin-deep
Beauty is its own reward

The proper study of mankind is never done
A woman's work is Man

An elephant may look at a king
A cat never forgets

Silence makes a wise head
A still tongue is golden

Those might make good themes for story-telling contests

Indeed: write a little collection of them, maybe only in my head, just for fun

In leafing through Jean Paul, that passage which seems to me to be the most consoling sentence in the German language: "Ye of little faith, look up! the primeval light is arriving!"

Good-byes and tips; the head receptionist and the gentle one, and by the red telephone the room maid. "I've had a wonderful time here," I say, "except that you never had the radio in my room repaired for me, and that I find hard to forgive!" "Yay!" says the head receptionist, with a fatherly shake of his head, yay, there was nothing wrong with the radio, all I had to do was stick in a tiny little paper clip, where it says "Antenna," just a teeny weeny paper clip, and it would've worked, and I ask how the devil, the dickens, in Heaven's name, was I supposed to know that, and the head receptionist gazes at me with a Hungarian hall porter's most fatherly smile and says in the mildest tone of reproach and with the most indulgent shake of the head betokening a thousand years of wisdom: "But Mr. F., one's supposed to know that

On the street, sudden machine-gun salvos: three youths are clacking the red balls, and the gentle receptionist explains that these are the last repercussions of the latest fad: tikki-takki, it was called, the tikki-takki ball game, and everyone, let me tell you, had been clacking, it had been just like during the war, tikki-takki, tikki-takki all over the place, tikki-takki even here in the hotel, a regular pest like the gypsies now, and in the end it had to be prohibited in public transport and restaurants, but it was all over now, there were only a few stupid boys who persisted in doing it

My last forints go to the sleeping-car conductor; he assesses them with his eyes and fingers and says, with a formal bow: "You will not be disturbed until you get to Berlin, sir

Once again, the stocky, almost trunkless apricot trees

The hills of Dömös from the other side

A miniature stone bridge over a little brook, arched, no bigger than a half-hoop, and a little pond with brown reeds and full of duckweed and, from the maize field beyond in the wind, a dull yellow veil of the brittle, pulverized remains of leaves

Define the position, your position; begin at the beginning; with yourself

Suddenly the landscape is interrupted by some brilliant green on a hill, and in the drab autumn and beyond the trotting of dun-colored pheasants I am amazed to see the exotically luscious, exuberant, fresh green of a cluster of young pine trees

This maelstrom, this emerald, this dynamic growth: never yet have I seen pine trees

Gone

Above gray rock overgrown with gray, ivy-like creepers, the gray trunks of the great beeches, and beyond the forest burns the field, the maize stubble is burning, the fire eats its way into the plain in long, slow, outward-curving lines, and yellow smoke, Apollyon's farewell, and along the edge of the field the ash and oak trees thick with mistletoe as if with nests of big, dangerous birds, and the sun slowly sinks into the fire, and the smoke turns gray

Farewell, Margit

Esztergom, evening sparkles, the broken bridges in the great, dark, sleeping river

Finished Madách, and I must laugh out loud on reaching the last line of this epic of humanity that is accused of pessimism: "Hear my words, O man, and fight on with confidence!"

Customs; border; passport; customs; passport; passport; customs; border; passport; customs; the duty officer (what substitute word do we have for "official"?) examines my customs declaration; as always, I have faithfully listed everything, all the titles of books, whether secondhand, newly acquired, or gifts from my colleagues, the plates, the replicas (two brooches, two pairs of cufflinks), two frames and a sweater for Barbara, a hooded sweater for Ursula, half a sausage, a little doll for Marsha, a head scarf, the bottle gourd from Dömös, a kilo of chestnuts, only one thing is not listed, the most precious: the secret of the Herz & Pick salami factory

Departure signals, German, loud, clear, punctual, although no one is getting on or off

The Elbe

Smoke

Birch trees

Monotonous pine forests. Lakes and sand

Pine trees

Approaching Schönefeld, the pond and the war memorial

Rummelsburg; Ostkreuz; Warschauer Street; entering the station; home

Cold; fog; the beloved North

To begin? Or: to end?